THE FEMALE
LEADERSHIP PARADOX

THE FEMALE LEADERSHIP PARADOX

POWER, PERFORMANCE, AND PROMOTION

MIRELLA VISSER
MANAGING DIRECTOR, CENTRE FOR INCLUSIVE LEADERSHIP

First published 2011 by
PALGRAVE MACMILLAN

Palgrave Macmillan in the UK is an imprint of Macmillan Publishers Limited,
registered in England, company number 785998, of Houndmills, Basingstoke,
Hampshire RG21 6XS.

Palgrave Macmillan in the US is a division of St Martin's Press LLC,
175 Fifth Avenue, New York, NY 10010.

Palgrave Macmillan is the global academic imprint of the above companies
and has companies and representatives throughout the world.

Palgrave® and Macmillan® are registered trademarks in the United States,
the United Kingdom, Europe and other countries.

ISBN 978–0–230–28920–8

This book is printed on paper suitable for recycling and made from fully
managed and sustained forest sources. Logging, pulping and manufacturing
processes are expected to conform to the environmental regulations of the
country of origin.

A catalogue record for this book is available from the British Library.

Library of Congress Cataloging-in-Publication Data
Visser, Mirella.
   The female leadership paradox : power, performance and promotion /
Mirella Visser.
      p.   cm.
   Includes index.
   ISBN 978–0–230–28920–8 (hardback)
   1. Women—Vocational guidance.   2. Leadership in women.
   3. Women executives—Promotions.   4. Career development.
   I. Title.
   HF5382.6.V57 2011
   658.4'092082—dc22   2011008500

10   9   8   7   6   5   4   3   2   1
20   19   18   17   16   15   14   13   12

Printed and bound in Great Britain by
MPG Group, Bodmin and King's Lynn

CONTENTS

LIST OF FIGURES AND TABLES

Figures

Tables

PREFACE

The number of conferences, networks, and initiatives aimed at increasing the number of women in top positions in our society has never been greater. Many CEOs in the corporate world have decided to implement diversity policies aimed at advancing women to leadership positions. Many changes have taken place in society and corporations to create more chances and choices for women. Many instruments have been developed to improve the likelihood of women reaching senior management functions. Nevertheless, the results are still seriously lagging behind the efforts and expectations. A pattern is emerging: women seem to perform a 'vanishing act' on their way to the top.

Purpose of this book

With this book I intend to contribute to improving the under-representation of women in top positions in our society through strengthening the collective knowledge of women and the organizations they work for. Women have become comfortable with sharing their personal career stories and addressing difficult questions such as: 'Are you prepared to make significant sacrifices to achieve your ambitions?' But we still need to refute myths such as 'If you work hard, you will get the promotion you deserve.' I hope that this book will not only stimulate the debate around this topic, but also provide practical tips and concrete advice for women on their way to the top.

Connecting FAQs and personal experiences

This book is based on a selection of the most frequently asked questions (FAQs) during workshops and lectures I have given on the topic of 'Women and Leadership'. It became clear to me that everywhere – from Amsterdam to Athens, from Berlin to Brussels, at universities, business schools, in companies, women's networks, clubs, and conferences – women are struggling with similar questions. The book also builds on my personal experiences as an international senior manager in the financial services industry and board member of companies and non-profit organizations. It is my intention to provide inspiration to address questions such as: 'What can you do to optimize the careers of women in the current circumstances?' and 'What crucial information is missing to make the step to senior management?' I challenge you to capitalize on all opportunities and not be sidelined as you wait for something to change in companies or society.

How to read this book

This book opens with two key questions: 'Do I consider myself a leader?' and 'Do I consider women as leaders?' At the heart of the book lies the *female leadership paradox*. The phenomenon of leadership as a masculine concept in our world today is a crucial factor in the development of women's leadership ambitions and skills. After all, if you don't see yourself or women in general as leaders, others won't see you as such either. You are the master and owner of your own career. Mobilizing your unique competencies prevents you from becoming a spectator on the sidelines watching what is happening around you – and with you. I challenge you to embrace a new positive metaphor to help shape your career, which I call *The Silk Road to the Top* (Chapter 8.1). Like the ancient trade routes connecting the East and the West and bringing prosperity to the world, the connection between women and men in leadership brings prosperity to our personal and business lives. The journey to the top in the business world is comparable to a journey to a faraway country. The new generation of women leaders has found different paths and has developed methods other than the traditional on their route to the top. Like silk, these paths are flexible, colorful, and sophisticated, and very different from those of traditional marching routes in the ancient pyramidal structures.

The metaphor of the Silk Road to the Top also refers to my personal experiences as a senior executive in Asia, working in different Asian cultures and in multicultural and multinational teams. My Silk Road to the Top so far has been characterized by often being the first and only woman in the management positions I have held. It has taught me that being open-minded and actively seeking to discover and embrace differences, in gender and in cultures, opens far more possibilities than I imagined before.

Pattern of power, performance, and promotion

From my analysis of the FAQs and my personal experiences, a pattern emerges which explains key bottlenecks in women's career advancement. Chapter 3 introduces the essential leadership competencies of *Power, Performance, and Promotion* that we need to develop strategically if we want to travel successfully. On our journey from operational manager to business leader, from junior through middle to senior management, the value of these competencies changes and requires us to adapt flexibly and purposefully.

Business case studies built on FAQs

After each discussion of a key theme, concrete business case studies based on the FAQs are described and analyzed, and a variety of strategies are proposed. These are daily situations women encounter in business. The business case studies have been built around the FAQs but do not reflect individual personal experiences at certain specific companies. They are generic. Some apply to women only, but others apply to all career makers, men and women.

I invite you to reflect on a wide variety of possible solutions, with the aim of finding the right approach for your individual situation – *the* ideal strategy does not exist because every situation is unique and requires a tailor-made approach. By further developing this approach, you will enhance your ability to make conscious choices yourself instead of having others make choices for you, which often leads to surprises and disappointments. Freedom of choice based on insight and knowledge will ultimately lead to more satisfaction and more direction in your career as leader.

This book is a testimony to my wish to promote more female and more balanced leadership in organizations. As such it embodies the connection between my personal experiences on the Silk Road and insights into this topic with those who asked the questions and with readers like you.

Your Silk Road

A successful strategy to the top consists of planning, developing the necessary tactics, and pursuing the right execution. Without a clear idea of direction your actions will lack focus and your career will depend largely on decisions made by others and a degree of luck. Inherent in action-planning is the ability to look ahead in order to preclude obstacles that hinder you. Looking ahead requires an open mind and the willingness to gather information and advice about your goals and the road ahead. How to achieve your goal should be defined in your tactic plan, which provides structure to execute your planned activities. Finally, a successful career strategy takes into account that unplanned events will have an impact on the course of your career. The flexibility to adapt the planning ensures that you will stay on track for your ultimate goal.

I invite you to use the book as a map to strategically plan your Silk Road to the Top.

Acknowledgments

My heartfelt gratitude goes out to all the courageous and open-minded women and men who discussed their personal dilemmas with me during various workshops, presentations, and discussions. I have been very privileged to meet you and I cherish the personal experiences we have shared.

Special thanks first of all to my partner, Fred Regoort, for his inspiration to write this book and in particular for his great sense of humor. My deep appreciation goes out to Nelleke Schoemaker and Frank Schreve for their invaluable advice and support over the years. I am very grateful for the encouragement of so many great people, in particular Hanneke van Dijk, Jessie Gordon, Paul-Peter Feld and Marguerite Soeteman-Reijnen. Special thanks also to my friend and former board colleague Annalisa Gigante, with whom I embarked upon my first book-writing project a few years ago (*Women on Boards – Moving Mountains*). Many thanks to my board colleagues and members of the European Professional Women's Network for their cooperation and friendship. Special recognition is due to the champions of women's leadership conferences, Isabella Lenarduzzi, Kristin Engvig, and Irene Natividad for their endeavors in promoting women's leadership. In addition, I would like to express my appreciation to so many I have been privileged to meet and work with over the years, in particular to Caf van Kempen, my fellow board members and members of the Works Council at Royal Swets & Zeitlinger. My sincere appreciation goes out to Pauline van der Meer Mohr, Theresa Firestone, Twan van de Kerkhof, Béatrice Guillaume-Grabisch, Fatima Ribeiro, Danica Purg, Julia Harrison, Vanessa Borchers and Elisabeth van Opstall, and Pim van Tol of Business Contact, who published the Dutch edition. I would also like to thank the members of the European Commission's Network of Women in Decision-making in Politics and the Economy for generously sharing their experiences and views over the years.[1] Finally, I would like to thank the 'group without a name', consisting of Daniëlle Balen, Astrid Belgrave, Nicolette Loonen-van Es, Mijntje Lückerath-Rovers, Bartje Schotman-Kruiten, Daniella Strik, Gwendolyn van Tunen, Chantal Verkooy, and Marijn Wiersma, for sharing the passion and sense of urgency to embark upon an ambitious project addressing the fundamental questions in restoring trust in the financial services sector.[2] A final word of thanks to Brigitt Albers, who is just starting her business, for designing the beautiful trailer for my book.[3] It has been a great Silk Road to the Top with all of you!

Mirella Visser
March 2011

CHAPTER 1

Seven Themes

1.1 FAQs

This chapter is an overview of the frequently asked questions (FAQs) that were posed during workshops, lectures, and individual conversations. They reflect the dilemmas women encounter in their careers. Some questions are self-evident, and women are actively looking for answers to these. Others are less obvious and only surface during an unexpected turn of events, as when a woman is passed over for a promotion or approached for a less-favored position. It appears that women do not always ask the right questions at the beginning of their career, which may lead to disappointments and surprises later on.

Most women at the start of their career do not expect that being a woman in a male-dominated business environment could ever become an issue. This perception gradually changes when they start competing with their male counterparts for the senior and most interesting functions. Many report that they seem to learn the tricks of the trade by just doing since they often lack information about the possible pitfalls on the way to the top.

1.2 Seven themes of leadership development

The FAQs are reproduced here using their original wording. They have not been embellished or rephrased in any way that alters their original meaning. They have been classified according to seven themes that are relevant to the development of our leadership competencies: *personal leadership, female leadership, frameworks and culture, power and politics, career, skills, and networking.*

Becoming a leader starts with our inner motivation – our *personal leadership* – or our drive to lead. The theme *personal leadership* addresses the basic question: 'What do I want to achieve and why?' The theme *female leadership* revolves around two inevitable questions: 'Does female leadership as such exist?' and 'If female leadership does exist, how does it influence our behaviors and perceptions of ourselves, and of other women as leaders?'

The questions based on *frameworks*, *culture*, *power*, and *politics* refer to the outside business world in which we operate. What are the rules of the game, and how can we succeed on the playing field?

The last three themes – *career*, *skills*, and *networking* – establish the 'connection' between our personal goals and the outside world in which we set out to achieve them. Which skills and competencies do we need in order to complete the Silk Road from junior to top management functions successfully?

Personal leadership

- Do I consider myself a leader?
- Can I stay authentic at the top?
- How do I keep a healthy work–life balance?
- Why should I have ambition?
- Why can I not express my ambition without being judged unpleasant?
- Should I be treated differently because I am a woman?
- Why do I meet resistance when I exercise power?

Female leadership

- Why are there so few women leaders?
- Do we take women leaders seriously?
- Do women really take different decisions?
- Are there specific feminine leadership qualities which help or hinder women in management positions?
- Do women not support each other or is this merely perception?
- Why would it be important to have more women at the top?

Frameworks and culture

- Why do so many women in my organization leave?
- What is wrong with corporate culture if there are no women in top management?
- Why am I treated as 'wife of' instead of business professional?
- Why do they address me as secretary or assistant?

- Why is it OK if my partner collects the children from school and not if I do?
- How do I manage cultural resistance?

Power and politics

- How do you cope with politics in an organization?
- I don't want power, but how can I still be successful in my career?
- Do women play politics differently than men?
- Why is someone else proposing my idea?
- Why am I not being heard if I present my idea to the management team?
- Why do they ask me to deliver bad news?
- Why do I suffer personal attacks?
- I don't like to play politics, but how can I still get the promotion I deserve?
- Why do I lose my job in the reorganization?
- How come some colleagues get away with everything?
- Why do I miss out on the most favored positions?

Career

- Why did I miss this promotion?
- Why do I not get the credit I deserve?
- Why do they always ask me for supporting instead of leading roles?
- Which courses or studies do I need to take?
- Why do they often approach me for difficult tasks?
- How do I successfully land a board position?
- Why do executive searchers never call me?
- Why is it so difficult to get back on track after a break?
- Why do I need to work so hard to get things done?
- How can I ensure to follow the career path which fits me best?

Skills

- Why do I not receive what I am asking for?
- Why do I get remarks about my appearance?

- How do I promote myself without provoking resistance?
- Why am I never the exception to the rule?
- Why do I earn less than my male peers?
- What do I say when I suddenly come across our CEO in the elevator?

Networking

- Why is networking so important?
- Do women network differently?
- Do I really need to take up golf?
- Why am I always the last one to know?
- Why am I losing good clients to colleagues?
- Why do I feel so uncomfortable at a business reception with all men in gray suits?
- Why do they decide for me?
- How do I build a strategic network?

The FAQs give an impression of the issues that women encounter on their way to the top. All questions are addressed in this book in various ways. Of course, this chapter is merely an overview of the questions I received, but my hope is that it will inspire you to pose more, other, and perhaps even better questions in order to discover new strategies for your leadership journey.

1.3 How to use the business case studies

Twenty business case studies have been developed from the FAQs. Each case study consists of three parts: the *Description*, the *Analysis*, and the *Strategies*.

The *Description* contains details of concrete events and behaviors. The case studies are set in different industries and companies in which the concrete events and behaviors seem to occur frequently. However, the case studies do not represent the situation found in all companies in any one industry.

The *Analysis* provides an overview of possible reasons for the outcome in each specific case study. Owing to the fact that every case study has multiple angles, and given that many reasons can contribute to the specific outcome of a case study, there is no single correct answer at any time. In the analysis, relevant patterns of behavior in women are discussed, based on my experiences and observations over the years. It is not my intention to classify all women by a few patterns, since behavioral differences between individual women are as large as between individual women and men, and between individual men. My goal is to clarify frequently observed patterns so that you can investigate how applicable they are to your personal situation.

The third part, *Strategies*, contains a number of suggestions and strategies to either prevent similar situations in the future or assist you in rewriting the script of the situations you encounter. In principle, you choose the strategy you feel most comfortable with. Nevertheless, in some cases the most comfortable strategy might actually be less effective than a less comfortable one. I challenge you to consider experimenting with less comfortable solutions. Enlarging your repertoire of skills and behaviors will enrich your leadership qualities in the long term, and thus will increase your chances of reaching a top position.

CHAPTER 2

Personal Leadership

2.1 What is driving you?

Leaders should regularly ask themselves 'What is driving me?' and 'What are my motives to lead?' We have become preoccupied with our curriculum vitae (CV). This overview of our educational background, the positions we have held, the responsibilities we have assumed, and the results we have achieved has become a 'this is me' statement. It reflects our progress, our professional direction, and may even provide indications about our future career. While a CV is a testimony of *what* we have done, it does not answer *why*. A CV does not address the following questions: Who are you as a leader? What kind of leader are you? Which values and principles underlie your actions and behaviors? Knowing the answers to these questions is crucial to ensuring that your career stays on course and that you are able to take decisions with integrity.

Key questions to ask about leadership are:

- How do you inspire people to follow you to reach a common goal?
- Why would people want to follow you?
- Why do you follow a leader?

In order to find meaningful answers to these questions and at the same time discover which qualities you consider to be indispensable in a good leader, you can read and complete Exercise 2.1.

Exercise 2.1

1. Identify five women whom you consider to be good leaders. Choose women who have proven to be effective leaders in the (business) environment in which you would like to be successful too.

2. Describe the three most important qualities of each woman you have identified. Make sure that your description is factual and based on displayed behaviors in concrete situations. A statement such as 'She is always so organized and efficient' is too general and should be further analyzed

and substantiated with examples of concrete behaviors. For instance: 'Her meetings never run late because she makes sure all issues on the agenda have been prepared well in advance', or 'She is always on time because she plans ahead for any traffic congestion and accidents', or 'People enjoy working with her because she encourages them to learn new things and she uses humor'. The advantage of analyzing concrete behaviors that make for a successful leader is that you can aspire to learn and adopt these behaviors yourself.

3. Compose a set of skills and behaviors which you consider to be indispensable for a good leader, based on the three most important leadership qualities of your five role models.

4. Repeat the exercise with examples of good male leaders in order to discover if your concept of good leadership is gender-neutral or gender-biased.

The outcomes of this exercise will provide you with sufficient insight to be able to develop and evaluate your effectiveness as a leader, and will give you confidence in the process.

2.2 Leadership parables

Discovering leadership stories and statements about leadership behaviors can provide a source of inspiration for the development of our own desired leadership style. Two of my favorite leadership parables follow.

The sound of the forest

One of the most beautiful stories about leadership I heard when living in Asia was the ancient story of a king who was preparing his son to take over his role in the future. The king sent his son to a leadership master who could teach him how to become a good leader. The master ordered the prince to travel to the nearby forest, listen to its sounds, and then report back on what he had heard. The prince eagerly headed for the forest and spent many hours carefully listening to all the different noises that emerged. Upon his return, he reported with great detail the sounds of the humming bees, the chirping crickets, the murmuring of the water in the creek, and the rustling leaves in the wind. He recalled the snorting noises of the wild boar and the ticking sounds of the woodpecker drilling away with its beak in the trunk of a tree.

But to the prince's great surprise the leadership master was not satisfied with his answers and commented that he had not listened carefully enough. The master sent him back to the forest to listen again. Disappointed about this first-time failure, the prince was determined to do better and so concentrated for a couple of hours to hear the sounds he must have missed. Despite his resolve, he did not discover any new or other sounds and gradually lost courage and confidence that he would ever be a good leader – until he finally rested beneath a tree, exhausted. Feeling relaxed, he surrendered to the surroundings. Suddenly, he was able to hear the 'inaudible': the sound of flowers opening in the sun, the sound of the sun warming the earth, the sound of the energy in the universe, and the sound of nothing. He realized that this was the sound of the forest the master must have meant. Indeed, upon his return his teacher explained that the ability to hear the inaudible is one of the core characteristics of good leaders. Leaders who are able to listen to the hearts of their people and hear their people's unspoken thoughts can address the unspoken needs and wishes, and inspire self-confidence. These leaders do not display ego-driven behaviors but are servants to the people they lead.

Inspiring people to long for the endless sea

Another, rather well-known story about the essence of leadership was written by Antoine de Saint-Exupéry.[1] A group of people had to build a ship that could transport them across the oceans to new countries and regions in the world. The leader engaged in finding the necessary building materials, developing a plan, describing the activities, and dividing the tasks between the team members. After a while the leader checked on the team's progress and found that the construction of the ship was way behind schedule and that the team was not functioning properly. He wondered why this was happening and started to interview each team member to find out what was causing the delay and lack of cooperation. It became clear that the leader had missed the most important component of leadership: a good leader starts with inspiring her or his team to long for the endless sea.

2.3 Your personal leadership statement

A personal leadership statement provides you with a clear direction for your leadership actions and behaviors. This statement is the creative expression of your intentions and motives to accept responsibility and of how you interact with your environment. It contains insights, statements, expressions, and quotes that resonate with you and which form the expression of your reasons to accept leadership responsibilities. A leadership statement is a snapshot of your motives and inspiration for your career at a particular moment. It will remain your guideline for a certain period of time until new insights and experiences need to be included. The next version of your leadership statement will be more refined and enriched in certain areas. One part of your statement will not be prone to adaptations: the part that contains your *basic values and principles*. The other parts will be more dynamic as you continuously learn from your experiences and adjust your vision on leadership based on feedback from peers and confidants. The process of developing a leadership statement results in not only the statement itself but also in an inner transformation, which will be reflected in your changed behavior. Your colleagues will notice that you lead from inner motives and personal integrity. This will enhance your credibility and effectiveness as a leader.

Exercise 2.2

1. Answer the following questions as a first step to developing your own concrete and precise leadership statement:

    ■ *What am I passionate about?*
    This question relates to the activities that fire you and which make your blood flow faster.

    ■ *Where can I make a valuable contribution?*
    You should know your talents and their worth. Without a clear picture of your strengths and the direction you like to deploy them in you will not be able to contribute to the best of your abilities; your contributions will then be random, coincidental, and arbitrary.

    ■ *What do I feel responsible for?*
    This question deals with your inner drive to take action. Without a certain sense of responsibility, ideas will remain ideas and will not materialize into concrete activities. Responsibility can be felt at different levels and for different issues. You may feel responsible for preventing staff redundancies during times of crisis and are therefore inspired to formulate and implement sustainable policies. Alternatively, you may be aware of a religious or worldly calling to leave a better world behind. A sense of responsibility can originate from values of justice and the conviction to combat discrimination.

2. Use the Internet, books, magazines, and your memory to recall texts, extracts, and quotations that reflect your inspiration to lead. In workshops, many participants discover that the three questions posed more or less automatically lead them to write down their personal leadership statement as a manifestation of their conscience and memory. This is not a coincidence but a process in which deeper unconscious intuition becomes conscious knowing.

3. Make a first attempt at writing a leadership statement. The test of a good leadership statement is that it feels natural when you articulate the sentences you have selected and that it builds up energy and strength toward the end. It provides power and inspiration for yourself and your audience. You should be able to remember the sentences easily because they reflect the core of what you define as good leadership.

Here is my personal leadership statement. It reproduces the inspiration from which I lead and my ambition to contribute to a profound shift in our society regarding the recognition and valuation of female leadership.

My leadership statement

- I am passionate about people, about developing their leadership talent, especially in women.
- I am fascinated by the concept of leadership and shocked by the absence of women in leadership.
- I am inspired by Mahatma Gandhi's words: `Be the change you want to see in the world.'
- I am guided by Madeleine Albright's sense of duty: `We have a responsibility in our time, as others have had in theirs, not to be prisoners of history but to shape history.'
- I am privileged to be a highly educated woman living in one of the most privileged parts of the world.
- At the same time I sometimes feel ashamed of this privilege and wonder if the absence of women in leadership has anything to do with this.
- I am accountable because I am part of the system; I am the system.
- Therefore, I am passionate about change, of myself first and foremost, and of the system, by striving for a more balanced leadership in society.

CHAPTER 3

Pattern of Power, Performance, and Promotion

Leadership starts with an ambition: an ambition to achieve a goal in a profession or an organization; an ambition to pursue lifelong learning; or an ambition to develop yourself and other people. Talent and a willingness to learn the necessary skills channel your ambition. Personal characteristics, such as perseverance and the ability to deal effectively with setbacks, determine if you will stay on course or drop out when the unexpected happens. In this chapter a model is introduced as a guideline for successful strategic career planning from operational manager to business leader.

3.1 The myth of meritocracy

From analysis of the frequently asked questions on which this book is based (see Chapter 1), a pattern emerges that gives insight into the reasons why many women often do not get the promotions they deserve or the positions they set out to achieve.

At the start of our career most of us assume that a good performance will more or less automatically lead to promotion and interesting functions. Women more so than men seem to be raised with the belief that meritocracy prevails and that you will be rewarded fairly for your efforts and achievements. The fact that large numbers of highly competent women with consistent excellent performance do not reach positions of power indicates that other components of leadership alongside performance might determine one's career success.

Successful women on the Silk Road to the Top do not rely exclusively on their excellent performance (*Performance*) while discharging their responsibilities. They strategically use the other crucial components of leadership, which are the ability to build and exercise influence through networking (*Power*) and the creation of a professional image through effective self-promotion (*Promotion*). Successful female leaders know how to devote attention to these three components in their leadership journey from junior to middle to senior to top management positions.

The workings of the pattern of power, performance, and promotion are often discovered (too) late in a career, when one of the components has received insufficient attention and the career stops or deviates from its original track. Because building power networks and a good reputation both take considerable effort and time, a shortage in one of these components is neither easily nor quickly repaired.

3.2 Focus on doing and details

In the beginning of our career at junior level we focus our attention on the correct execution of the tasks assigned to us in line with our job description (performance-related activities). We strive to carry out our tasks efficiently, with an eye for detail, in order to reach our goals. How well we perform these tasks defines how our performance will be judged by our superiors. A straightforward example is the sales target of a sales representative to recruit 5 new clients every month and render personalized service to 20 existing clients, selling 10 of them extra services.

At junior level it is essential to acquire crucial knowledge and management skills. The focus is on education, training, and gaining experience for the execution of the role, such as overall company knowledge, and specialist product and market expertise. In this process perfectionism and attention to detail are prevalent. Unsatisfactory performance can be addressed through extra specialist training and on-the-job training. For example, if an individual fails to meet sales targets due to insufficient communication skills, toward clients or the organization, specific training can help that individual to improve his or her sales performance.

Competition for promotion from junior levels to more senior levels is based on performance. The first people to receive a promotion will tend to be the ones who outperformed others on their measurable targets. This initial experience seems to confirm for many the myth of meritocracy.

In the junior phase the aspects of power and promotion receive little attention. Networks primarily consist of personal contacts, such as friends and family, and provide social and emotional support. Self-promotion does not take place systematically or strategically and is aimed at promoting specific results in the job.

An excellent track record on performance is a prerequisite for development to middle and, later, senior management. Without such a track record, the other components of successful leadership will be obsolete.

3.3 Focus on delegation

In the development phase from junior to middle manager the almost exclusive focus on the execution of tasks shifts gradually and partially toward the competencies associated with power and promotion. The ability to handle difficult issues, deliver exceptional performance when needed, and develop new ideas and sources (e.g. clients) becomes more important.

In this phase, you learn to work through others instead of completely relying on yourself to execute your tasks. This requires the development of delegation skills based on self-confidence as a leader and the ability to trust and empower others. In addition, you need to have access to necessary information about people and resources that can be used for the tasks at hand. Having access to formal and informal networks is a prerequisite for success. The relevant networks will primarily consist of contacts within your organization which the middle manager can use to locate and unlock internal resources. Being part of the internal and informal networks also ensures that difficulties in the execution of your tasks will be prevented and conflicts resolved quickly.

Successful middle managers experience the power of networking (*Power*) and recognize that networking is an increasingly important tool to improve their effectiveness in reaching their goals. Consequently, the time spent in building and maintaining these networks will grow with its importance.

In this phase the third aspect of successful leadership – the ability to communicate consistently and professionally about your achievements (*Promotion*) – gains importance too. You start to proactively develop activities that promote both your personal successes and those of your team. Reputation and image building are mainly aimed at your own organization and ensure that people are aware of your work. The emphasis is not on creating an image per se, but on creating a reputation as a professional and excellent leader in your company.

A common pattern in the career development of women is that they remain concentrated on the execution of their tasks, aiming for more than 100 per cent perfection in middle-management functions. The tendency to *dot all the i's and cross all the t's* may result in a low degree of delegation and, consequently, an increasing pressure to perform. In this 'overachievers' mode, women feel that they lack energy and time to devote to the other two essential competencies of power and promotion. In addition, they may underestimate the value of these components for their career advancement. The consequence may well be that career development falls behind while one is working even harder and putting in more hours than before.

3.4 Focus on directing

On the career path from middle to senior management the individual differences in education, training, experience, and technical expertise become less determining. A good reputation and a network of powerful contacts are prerequisites for senior functions. Of good senior managers employees say that they offer ample learning opportunities in a stimulating environment. Their departments or projects are among the most interesting and influential ones and, therefore, attract the best talents. Good leaders inspire their followers not only by delegating tasks and responsibilities but also by *directing different disciplines* to work together as a whole for the good of the company.

The transition to top management positions requires excellent skills in the areas of power and promotion. Their significance gradually shifts from an operational to a strategic level when you move from operational manager to business leader. They reinforce each other in the build-up of your 'political capital': your reputation to get things done and have a network of support and recognition. Sufficient political capital enables you to set the agenda and to influence the desires of others.

The company's internal networks remain important for accessing resources and information in the organization in order to execute operational tasks and prevent and resolve conflicts. Next to these networks, new networks extend into external contacts outside the company, such as shareholders, financial markets, trade organizations, interest groups, and competitors. The information coming from these networks provides crucial knowledge for the strategic aspects of a senior management role. Information about market trends, competitors' activities, and new products, for instance, enables the senior manager to develop a long-term strategic vision for the organization. Often, the external networks give access to qualified candidates at other organizations for important senior functions at your company. It is important to find informal networks that may provide a confidential platform to discuss strategic or sensitive issues. In these networks, confidentiality and reciprocity prevail and they become indispensable sounding boards to test arguments and develop tactics.

One of the biggest challenges for top managers is to organize their own critics. Informal connections with leaders of other organizations fulfill an important role in this crucial process. The distance and the level of confidentiality ensure that a leader can safely discuss even the most difficult issues without having to involve his or her organization. Good leaders actively seek out opportunities, both within and outside of their

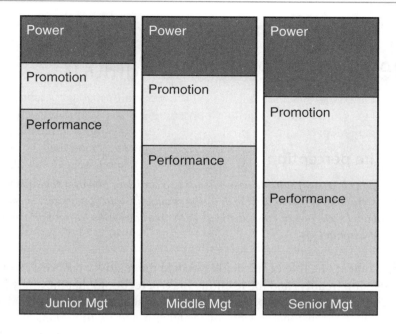

Figure 3.1 Pattern of power, performance, and promotion

organization, to provide them with feedback on their personal behavior and strategic information for the development of their vision.

The progress from junior through middle and senior to top managerial level takes place over many years. Women who have the ambition to achieve a top position need to strategically build and expand their networks and promotion activities in order to reach their goal. It is crucial to consciously allocate sufficient time to the three different competencies and prevent the common mistake of getting stuck in perfectionism in performance.

Senior management means focusing on 'doing the right things' instead of 'doing things right', which is the focal point in junior managerial roles. This runs parallel with the difference between being a manager and being a leader. Instead of working harder, you learn to work smarter by building power networks and developing an excellent reputation.

Figure 3.1 demonstrates the necessary shift in time and relative importance of the competencies of power, performance, and promotion during the transition from junior to senior management. The Summary Schedule at the end of this book provides the connection between the FAQs and the pattern of power, performance, and promotion.

CHAPTER 4

The Female Leadership Paradox

4.1 The perception

A paradox is a set of statements that leads to a contradiction or a situation which defies intuition. It is also used to describe situations which are merely surprising or ironic. Often, one of the statements in the paradox is based on half-truths or biased assumptions.

In this context, the title of this book refers to the relative absence of women in leadership (reality) and the resulting bias (perception) that they may have a general inability to be successful leaders. It also refers to the ambivalence women have toward the concept of leadership and its important elements of power and ambition. The title aims to defy the common notion that the under-representation of women in leadership is 'simply the way it is'. There is no reason to question women's ability to lead. Last, but not least, the title refers to the phenomenon, described in this chapter, that, often, the presence of feminine qualities in male leaders makes them great leaders and the same is true the other way round.

This chapter addresses the relationship between women and leadership. How does the absence of realistic female role models affect the image women have of leaders and of themselves as leaders? How does this image influence career choices and motivations to strive for a leadership position? Why is it so important to improve the numbers of women in decision-making positions in our society and our organizations?

Leadership experiment

During the workshops and conferences I asked the audience the following questions: 'If you think of leadership, which name comes to mind immediately?' and 'Who do you consider to be a good leader?' Regardless of the composition of the audience, which included students, directors, managers, women, and/or men, the following distribution in responses was universal.

Of the leaders whose names were called out spontaneously, 95 percent were men, among which Nelson Mandela was the most popular. Other popular leaders were Barack Obama, Richard Branson, Mahatma Gandhi, Jack Welch, a few soccer players, some teachers at school, and trainers at the sports club.

Women's names were mentioned in just 5 percent of cases. Popular female leaders were Madeleine Albright, Mother Teresa, Angela Merkel, Margaret Thatcher, and Hillary Clinton. Less frequently mentioned were Aung San Suu Kyi, female royalty, 'my own mother', and other female relatives, such as aunts and grandmothers who had played an important role in the respondents' youth.

Occasionally at a meeting, one of the male participants would stand up and make the point that he considered himself to be a good leader. In one case only, at a conference with more than 400 female participants, a woman came forward claiming she was a good leader; she received a standing ovation from the audience.

Leadership is a masculine concept

The results of the leadership experiment confirm that the concept of leadership in our society is a masculine construct. This experience is the same for men and women. Women who are aware of this phenomenon actively seek female role models. They are able to mention the names of more female leaders than women who are unaware and who proclaim that the discussion about male and female leadership is irrelevant.

The good leader's paradox

Discussions following the leadership experiment revealed that next to traits such as strength, courage, and integrity especially, typical feminine leadership qualities were responsible for rating leaders as 'good leaders'. Qualities such as empathy, the ability to connect with people, kindness, and mildness were frequently mentioned. In addition, good leaders were judged to have excellent communication skills.

In 1990 Judy Rosener was the first author who investigated how women managers behaved. The characteristics she described still form the basis of our current thinking about feminine leadership qualities.

Feminine traits: friendly, emotional, caring, supportive, sensitive, empathic, dependent.

Masculine traits: dominant, aggressive, strong, autocratic, analytical, competitive, independent.

Discussion with/against Collinson & Hearn (1996) in Bradley (?) The Myths of Work p 79:2

The positive evaluation of the feminine leadership qualities in male role models is in contrast to the much-heard criticism of one of the most appealing female leaders, Margaret Thatcher. Despite the fact that she is retired from the public eye, generations still regard her as a good example of a female leader. Although many admired her drive and ability to hold her own among male politicians, she was fiercely criticized for her behavior, which was dominated by her masculine qualities and gave her the nickname 'The Iron Lady'. Other popular role models of female leadership, for example Mother Teresa and Aung San Suu Kyi, personify not only the feminine traits of care and sacrifice, but also the masculine leadership qualities of strength and courage to address situations of injustice.

It is important to keep in mind the female leadership paradox during discussions about women and leadership, and feminine leadership, because it greatly influences the prevailing concepts that both men and women have of leadership. The effect on women may be that they experience the concept of leadership as an alien phenomenon with which they cannot spontaneously identify. The absence of an abundance of positive role models of female leaders in our society only confirms this experience. The effect on men may be that they do not take women leaders seriously, consciously or subconsciously, and that they accept the absence of women leaders as normal and as it should be.

4.2 Do you consider women as leaders?

Research has been conducted about the way women perceive other women as leaders. A study by Harvard University[1] investigated if professional women experienced other women as positive role models. The research found that women in organizations with few female employees are less inclined to experience their gender as a positive basis of identification with other women. In these organizations, senior women are hardly recognized as legitimate role models for top positions. In addition, these women experience more competition and low levels of support from other women in the organization.

Status counts

The status of the group one belongs to is of vital importance. Employees belonging to a group with low status in an organization, such as women in an organization with few female employees, will more often use behaviors that are conducive to improving their own situation, even if this behavior could have a destructive effect on the status of the whole group. When differences in status between men and women in an organization become larger and reflected in the numbers of men and women in crucial positions, the chance that working relationships between women will be affected negatively increases.

The explanation for this can be found in the way we react to our so-called social identity. In case the group to which we belong has low status in an organization (like women in some), individual female employees will be inclined to assert themselves even at the expense of other members of the group. When the group numbers increase and the group's status improves, individuals will be more comfortable relying on the group for their advancement, and solidarity among its members will grow accordingly.

The informal circuit enhances status

In highly politicized organizations, your status also depends on being part of networks of important people. Their status reflects on all the members of the group. In companies in which women have lower status than men, women often report difficulty in becoming part of important informal channels. The impact on their careers can be significant because they may miss out on crucial information and may, consequently, be less effective in the execution of their tasks.

How to measure women's status in organizations

There is a simple test to get an impression of the status of women within an organization. Companies that have relatively low levels of women in senior positions compared to their overall participation convey the message, deliberately or unconsciously, that career opportunities for women are limited. Next to the absolute numbers of women in senior management, another important indicator of the status of women is the type of position these women hold. In organizations where women are primarily found in supporting and caring roles, in communications, facilities management, relationship-building, and external representation, the perception of limited career chances is significantly reinforced. Organizations with adequate numbers of women in senior management roles in the 'heart of the business', for example in business unit management, often with profit and loss responsibilities, or in roles of strategic importance, are giving the right message.

Solitary or solidarity

In companies in which line-management positions and functions with bottom-line responsibility are prerequisites for obtaining status, women in supporting roles often struggle with their status and, consequently, solidarity among women suffers. When men and senior women are regularly confronted with the absence of solidarity of female employees, their already relatively low status spirals further downwards. Unaware of the described patterns of behavior caused by the psychological impact of our social identity, male managers will evaluate women's lack of solidarity as unprofessional and not constructive. From their perspective as high-status employees, women's behaviors may destroy the atmosphere of cooperation in the company.

Cooperation challenges

Women are often more critical of women leaders because they are simply not used to women operating in senior positions. There are very few situations, especially in top management, in which women are led by a woman. Many women in senior positions report that their authority is less likely to be accepted by their female than by their male colleagues. Because situations in which a woman leads other women are rare, they are likely to attract more-than-average attention from the environment. It becomes immediately clear when problems arise in the cooperation between women.

One of the important functions of women's networks is that members have the opportunity to experience working in all-women teams. The dynamics of these organizations are often quite particular and demand specific skills and qualities from their female leaders.

Occupational segregation

In occupations in which feminine qualities such as care and compassion are core qualities, for instance in nursing, belonging to the group of women may have more positive than negative consequences. Often, a more balanced distribution is observed (in health care organizations, more than half of managers are women); at the same time destructive behavior toward the group is less prevalent than in organizations characterized by few women in senior positions.

Lowering our expectations of women leaders

This collection of factors has an important consequence. If women consistently receive the message that lower status positions are theirs and higher status positions are reserved for their male peers, they will gradually, unconsciously, lower their expectations of themselves and of their female colleagues. Achieving an important position will be deemed to be (nearly) impossible. Women who aim to break out of this pattern will not be accepted by the men in the group nor by the women outside of the group.

This subtle but comprehensive process of lowering our expectations of women leaders in our society is one of the most important causes for the stagnation of fundamental change in the gender of leadership. Some women seem to have internalized to be unfit for leadership and are supported in this conviction by men and women alike; a real 'catch 22' for the brave ones who try to beat the odds.

It starts with education

Unfortunately, the underutilization of women's full talents is not addressed in the current educational system and at universities and business schools in particular. Some business schools are conducting experiments with the composition of the working groups in which students work together to pre-pare papers and complete assignments. Since on average 15–25 percent of MBA class students nowadays are women, often they are spread across the groups. Consequently, most of them will be in a minority position and often the only woman in the working group.

Competition creates collective insecurity

In one of the MBA experiments, a number of all-female groups were com-posed, next to perfectly balanced groups (50/50 men/women) and all-male groups. The female students, who had grown used to their exceptional status of minority in the groups, were suddenly confronted with a new situation. In a group with only women they had to compete with the other groups for the highest ratings in class. This experience created anxiety in many of them, with the exception of the American students who attended one of the women's colleges of the Seven Sisters Colleges.[2] The usual informal tone in their conversations became affected by the element of competition. Although the individual scores of the women in the women's groups were far above the average for the class, most of them believed that their group would not perform as well as the mixed and all-male groups. Some women who were placed in a women's group experienced this as a demotion and a degradation of their status in class. None of the men placed in an all-male group reported a similar experience. Because of fierce resistance from the women, the experiment was cut short, in some cases in order to prevent damage to the students' motivation to complete the MBA.

These experiments show that still some of our young, highly educated women (25–35 years) with international work experience and ambition to follow an MBA do not have full confidence in their own abilities and those of their fellow female students. Without openly addressing this implicit self-censorship during their studies, these women will enter their career paths with a potential collective inferiority complex, which might hinder them along the way.

Ambivalence in ambition

Ambition is based on your knowledge and experience on the one hand and on the recognition and appreciation of your work by the environment on the other hand. It is a widespread and persistent myth that women lack ambition to reach a top position. Of course, not all women strive for this goal, nor do all men. Many studies have shown that highly educated women and men share similar levels of ambition. The difference primarily lies in the way men and women rate success (realization of your ambitions) and in the way they verbalize their goals.

A common pattern seen in the business world is that women's career motives predominantly consist of *inner drives*. The content of the position and the opportunities to grow and develop their skills seem to have priority. In addition, women like to be recognized as experts in their field and to have a balanced lifestyle, with sufficient time for family responsibilities and activities such as sports, courses, and voluntary work.

Men more often than women make career choices based on *external motives*, such as the place in a formal hierarchy, status of a position, salary, and fringe benefits, including the location and size of their office, brand of car, memberships of clubs, and so on. Of course, these general statements do not apply to all individual employees. Nevertheless, one of the main reasons why women in general negotiate less frequently for salary raises and promotions is closely related to their inner motivations to accept a position in the first place.

Vanishing act of women on their way to the top

Receiving little recognition for your talents has an undermining effect on your ambition and often leads to the lowering of your expectations for the future, consciously or unconsciously. This process takes place in many women's careers because they have to operate in an environment in which the level of one's salary and challenging high-profile tasks are the proof of one's worth and status, and the equivalent of recognition in this world. The so-called vanishing act of women on their way to the top in large corporations is largely due to women being underpaid, often without being aware of the fact, and feeling undervalued.

4.3 How women leaders lead

Do women really lead differently than men? Or is it perception only? Do women have other motives to aspire to power?

Women score differently than men on certain leadership qualities. Women leaders more often use participative and democratic styles and pay more attention to interpersonal relationships. Women who display typical masculine traits, such as directive and autocratic behaviors, are judged as less effective than men who display these behaviors. This is primarily caused by the expectations men and women have with regard to effective leadership.

A meta-study,[3] which analyzed the results of a large number of similar studies, showed that despite the differences in behavior of male and female leaders, both were as effective, generally speaking. Effectiveness depends more on the individual with his or her specific behaviors than on gender-specific traits.

Happy workers

In a recent study about the impact of female supervisors on job experiences, health,[4] and well-being of their subordinates both men and women reported positive effects. Next to higher levels of mastery and social support at work, the workers experienced less conflict with work–life balance and felt less depressed.

Role models

Choosing a role model is a personal decision. Three of my favorites are listed below.

I do not bang my fist on the table. My way is to think, consult, and then decide. I think people still have to get used to the leadership style of a (an East German) woman.[5]

Angela Merkel, Chancellor of Germany

If you want anything said, ask a man. If you want anything done, ask a woman.

Margaret Thatcher, former Prime Minister
of the United Kingdom

My inspiration for this fascinating work is to contribute to creating a better future.[6]

Neelie Kroes, European Commissioner
for Competition (2009)

Missing vision?

A recent study among the alumni of a business school concluded that women score the same or better than men on nine out of ten leadership competencies, which would show women are actually better leaders.[7] On one competency men outperformed women: vision, defined as the ability to pick up new opportunities and trends in the environment and to set a new strategic direction for the enterprise. The title of the article, 'Women and the Vision Thing', clearly emphasizes the mere 10 percent of competencies on which women scored lower instead of emphasizing the 90 percent on which women achieved similar or better scores than the surveyed male leaders. In addition, the value attributed to the competency of 'developing a vision' again positions women implicitly as less successful leaders than men.

Perception or reality?

One of the explanations for women's perceived insufficient visionary capabilities is the fact that many use different mechanisms to develop their vision. Their often more participative and democratic leadership styles prompt women leaders to actively solicit the input from others when developing their vision for the strategic direction of an organization. In some business cultures this behavior is interpreted as weakness.

Another possible reason for this alleged insufficiency in visionary abilities is that women may be less comfortable promoting a vision as their personal vision than men, because it may present risks they would rather avoid.

A last possible explanation is that women do not discard the importance of a clear direction for an organization, but are reluctant to give it more attention than is needed. Interestingly, visionary capabilities can be learned, so one can expect that the differences in this area will disappear in time.

Symbol of significant change

If we define the essence of leadership as 'having followers', history provides many examples of women who became 'the voice of the people' yearning for change in their society.[8] They became the symbol of a fundamental political shift by taking up leading positions in situations giving evidence to the consensus that had built up for a radically different approach. In those societies women leaders fulfilled the role of catalyst and change agent. A well-known example is opposition leader Aung San Suu Kyi in Myanmar (Burma).

In Asia, gender stereotyping has proved to create a political advantage for women.[9] As well as in Myanmar, women have led successful popular uprisings against dictators in Bangladesh, Indonesia, Pakistan, the Philippines, and Malaysia. Interestingly, these women leaders derived their leadership status from male martyrs, as their widows, wives, and daughters. Being part of the weaker sex labeled women as non-violent. They were not perceived as a threat and were therefore better equipped in uniting opposition and becoming the voice of the oppressed people.

The glass cliff

Women leaders' special status as change agents in the political world seems to have found an equivalent in a new phenomenon in the business world, called the glass cliff. Researchers at Exeter University concluded that more women than men get appointed to high-risk positions.[10] The companies in the research recorded significantly lower results in the months preceding the appointment of a female top manager than their peer group companies led by male top executives. The experiment pointed toward women being the preferred choice when a company is in trouble. Despite the positive connotation this may have on the surface, it may well be a glass cliff that women fall from. Women are often not part of the informal networks and may consequently be missing the crucial, sensitive information needed for a proper assessment of the risks when accepting a certain position. Often, women are being approached for high-risk roles after men have turned them down because of reputational risk and because they often have more offers to choose from. Therefore, the development that the number of women leading companies that are in financial difficulty or are otherwise in turmoil cannot straightforwardly be interpreted as positive. It may well be the precursor of a new form of discrimination, the glass cliff.

4.4 The importance of women in top positions

The viewpoints about the absence of women in top positions are primarily determined by cultural motives and are therefore subject to change. In the 1960s and 1970s the topic was predominantly dealt with as part of the emancipation movement, using human rights and moral arguments. Nowadays the prevailing arguments are more linked to the effectiveness of an organization and the benefits that can be achieved. This way of thinking runs parallel with new insights about the core competencies and the creation of competitive advantage of companies and organizations. The drawback has been that in many companies, as is shown in the very slow progress of women in senior positions, the topic of diversity is primarily used for PR purposes. Management's true intentions around this theme are reflected in the way the company's diversity strategy is tied to the overall strategy, in how the policy is translated into concrete measurable results, and in the weight of the role and level of responsibility of diversity officers.

Ten prevailing perspectives on the importance of a better balance of men and women in top positions follow.

1 Equal representation

There is no reason why the composition of our population, 50 percent men and 50 percent women, should not be reflected at all levels of society. This argument of 'equal representation' is primarily used by governments in connection with the legitimacy of decision-making in a democracy. Governments that take the principles of democracy, non-discrimination, and equal representation seriously actively strive for gender equality at ministerial level and in parliament. This responsibility follows from the principles as a natural responsibility. Voluntary or legislated quotas to achieve this goal are used when the natural process does not result in equal representation at the democratic bodies.

Companies are starting to use the argument of equal representation too, but for different reasons than democratic principles. Especially when their target markets consist of more than 50 percent women, it is considered important that not only male customers are represented at top levels but also female customers. A successful company should reflect its customer groups at all levels in order to respond quickly to all customer demands.

2 Legitimacy of power

The argument that women should be part of the center of power can be driven by the principle that decisions in society can only have legitimacy if all relevant groups take equal part in the process. In our democratic society this principle means that only decisions that are taken by bodies in which men and women are equally represented at decision-making level are legitimate and therefore supported by the public. In this theory the legitimacy and acceptance of decisions are dependent on sufficient representation of the various communities in the decision-making bodies. Finland, the only European country where government consisted of 60 percent women and 40 percent men in 2010, applies the principle of the legitimacy of power as the foundation of the democratic institutions that represent the people. The underlying principle or conviction in Finnish society is that men and women hold not only equal rights toward decision-making, but also equal competencies (intelligence and experience) to fully participate in the decision-making processes.

The argument of the legitimacy of power is primarily used by governments and (semi-) governmental institutions and bodies as a principle of equal representation in a democracy. Companies often wave aside this argument by explaining that they are not a democratic body and that commercial entities require a different set of rules. Their prevailing principle is 'to have the right person for the job'. Applying the legitimacy principle through legislated quotas could well, in this school of thought, lead to promoting less qualified people to crucial positions in the decision-making processes. Companies using this argumentation implicitly communicate that they believe that there is a lack of sufficiently qualified women for top positions.

3 Combating discrimination

The purest form of striving for equality starts with the belief that men and women are equal in value and should therefore receive equal treatment. This is different from the beliefs held in the 1960s, when women and men were deemed to be 'the same'. Nowadays it is a common belief that men and women are not alike or identical but equal in value. The right to not be discriminated against is laid down in our constitution and international treaties. It is deemed unacceptable if women get discriminated against for leadership positions. Despite the proof in the statistics, many companies are convinced that the low numbers of women in senior management are not the result of discrimination but of other factors. They defy gender discrimination by appointing a special officer responsible for investigating cases of discrimination and harassment. Implicit and subconscious discrimination, however, are difficult to discover.

4 The female advantage or celebrating femininity

This argumentation is based on the premise that women have something extra to add and that female leadership qualities at the top level of an organization contribute to better-quality decision-making. In this vision all women are seen as the embodiment of positive female competencies, such as empathy, care, and a cooperative attitude. These qualities are in sharp contrast to the masculine ones that are dominating the top levels of organizations, such as result orientation, business focus, and even 'macho behaviors'. Value judgments about feminine and masculine competencies are driving this vision. The implicit assumption that women are better at these particular feminine qualities may lead to their over-representation in positions in which those qualities are crucial, for instance the supporting, facilitating, and communicative roles.

Organizations that typecast women according to this vision will experience difficulty in advancing them to top positions because the route to the top is generally not paved with these types of roles. Female employees with a healthy mix of masculine and feminine competencies will avoid working for such an organization because they will anticipate being groomed for specific feminine roles at one point in their career. Women who aspire to have end responsibility or to lead challenging business units will feel less comfortable and undervalued in the more traditional roles in HR management, PR, and communication.

This method of thinking ignores the conclusions from academic research pointing out that both men and women have feminine and masculine qualities and that none of these clusters would be more valuable or more effective than the other. This way of celebrating femininity often results in creating a clear contrast with the male-dominated business world. Victimization and the notion that women's 'better' leadership style is being boycotted by others may occur. Some women's organizations, conferences, and networks place emphasis on the celebration of feminine qualities. It strengthens both the collective and individual feelings of self-worth. In these situations, women are supported in their perception of their good qualities and in their 'battles' against the (perceived or real) male dominance. This important psychological effect can also be observed in groups or clubs of people with other distinguishable characteristics who share a common goal (weight loss, sharing experiences) and support each other in achieving their common goals.

5 Talent pool management

This argument for a gender-balanced top management builds on the notion that top talents are prevalent among women and men in the same way. There is equality in terms of competencies and ability to serve in leading roles. Organizations that strive to develop talent to the full in order to fulfill their critical positions with top candidates formulate and execute policies to enlarge the pool of available talent. This approach increases the chance that indeed only the best talents will reach the top of the organization. An important additional argument for this school of thought can be found in the demographic development of the ageing population in the developed world. This will lead not only to the current retirement age being postponed, but also to the need to increase female labor force participation.

PR value

Few organizations oppose the argument of the necessity to use all talents available, and many have even formulated proactive policies to this end. However, the disappointingly low numbers of women in senior positions show that effective measures to optimize the use of all talents are not yet in place. Among reasons cited for this lack of progress are the organizational culture which does not accept women in those roles, the absence of successful female role models, the composition of selection and nominating committees for promotions, and the unconscious biases in the selection procedures, to name a few. The need to use all talents available has become one of the most frequently used arguments by CEOs, HR directors, and diversity officers. It is a positive, sympathetic message and harbors a clear willingness toward promoting women to senior roles. Despite the popularity of the argument, the absence of proven effective policies and instruments to make change happen has gradually turned it from a beautiful slogan into mere lip service with primarily PR value.

Companies that consider the strategy to appoint more women in senior positions as one of talent management will allocate responsibility for it to the HR department. It depends on the status of the HR function and the power of the individual HR employee if consistent policies will be developed and concrete results achieved. Since in most organizations the role of the HR department is of a more advisory than decision-making nature, the implementation of concrete measures may be slowed down or not even get off the ground when human resources is driving the process.

Norwegian example of quota legislation

The need to ensure a steady and sufficient supply of labor in an increasingly competitive world was the leading principle in the Norwegian quota legislation for company boards, which was announced in 2003. As from January 1 2009 the boards of listed companies (around 500) should consist of at least 40 percent men and at least 40 percent women (applicable to boards of ten persons or more).[11] Violation will lead to certain penalties, ranging from official warnings to correct the situation to fines and, ultimately, delisting of the company (removal from the Norwegian Stock Exchange). The law, which was introduced by the Minister of Trade and Industry, was carefully drafted and was the logical continuation of the first quota law of 1987 for gender balance in boards of governmental bodies and committees. The 1987 law resulted in a representation of 44 percent women on these boards.

Decades of active government policies to support families removed many obstacles in the workplace in Norway. The visibility of large numbers of women in senior governmental roles led to a wider acceptance by the public of women leaders in general. Gradually, common beliefs in society transformed and women with a higher education were expected to continue their careers in the same way as men, and jointly combine the tasks of raising children. Critics have said that these family-supporting measures and facilities have become a significant financial burden for companies and have led to small- and medium-sized companies becoming more reluctant to hire young women.

Despite the supportive family policies it became clear in 2007 that the advancement of women had taken place primarily in the public sector. Political and media pressure, especially on the larger companies to improve their track record, were not successful. CEOs complained that there was a lack of qualified women to fulfill the board positions. Shareholders opposed the implementation of the quota legislation fiercely, citing the violation of their right to choose and appoint the best candidates to their boards. Companies seemed to be reluctant to drive change voluntarily. In preparation of the implementation of the quota law in 2009, the Norwegian government, together with the corporate sector and employers' federations, organized a variety of activities aimed at identifying and developing female leadership potential. In 2009 the share of women on Norwegian companies' boards (largest quoted companies) reached 42 percent, which is testimony to the success of the multidisciplinary approach and the introduction of serious penalties.[12] Interestingly, Sweden and Finland recorded 27 and 24 percent respectively without implementing rigorous quota legislation.

6 Corporate social responsibility

Recently, the argument of corporate social responsibility has become a popular new angle in the debate to increase the representation of women in senior management. Organizations have gradually become aware that they should not only take the interests of shareholders and employees to heart, but also contribute to society as a whole and act like a responsible citizen. Companies are finding that the public increasingly judges them on the way they fulfill their social duties. A clear and consistent policy to promote women to senior management positions is one of the instruments being used to fulfill this social responsibility. This type of company may well choose to report on the progress of its diversity policies in the corporate social responsibility annual report or in a special section of the annual report.

The disadvantage of the use of the corporate social responsibility argument is that in times of economic downturn these activities are among the first ones to suffer budget cuts. In addition, corporate social responsibility has not (yet) been widely accepted as a core strategy and competency of a company, whereas the topic of the representation of women at the top level should be embedded as such in the company's strategy.

Individual social responsibility

The other side of the coin is that women themselves are being questioned more frequently about their responsibility toward society, too. Is part-time work, often at lower levels than your competency, an acceptable career for a highly educated woman? Some call into question the acceptability of the high costs for society if women do not make good use of their training. After all, a university education is costly and substantially subsidized by government funds, which have been derived from taxation. Some politicians have even come out in favor of reclaiming (part of) the tuition fees in extreme cases when no use is made of university education at all. In times of spending cuts and limitations on the number of university places (numerus fixus), which make it more difficult to be accepted for the study of choice, the pressure on women who do not use their qualifications to contribute to society will undoubtedly increase further.

7   The business case

Nowadays the most popular way of proving the added value of women in senior positions in companies is to present the so-called business case. This provides all arguments and underlying numbers linked to the strategic goals of the organization. Starting from the company's mission statement and strategy, the business case contains an analysis of the ways a diverse workforce can contribute to the realization of the set goals.

The business case is built on a macro-economic analysis of the developments in the labor market. The impact of the ageing population further demonstrates the need to *recruit, develop, and retain female talent*. If the company will not be able to ensure a pipeline of qualified employees it is likely to seriously compromise its competitiveness in the longer term.

Another prevailing argument in the business case is the *marketing and sales perspective* of being close to your customers. Companies with a large female customer base consider it a business issue to have female employees involved in all decision-making structures. This will better equip them to design new products and deliver new services since they mirror the market. In addition, female customers are increasingly looking at the composition of top management before deciding on purchases.

Other frequently used arguments in the business case relate to the company's *corporate social responsibility* policies, requiring the representation of all communities in the company's management structure.

Lastly, achieving an image of *preferred employer* has become increasingly important for companies and a driving factor in the appointment of visible women to top layers of the organization.

Frequently used models to demonstrate financial benefit include a calculation of the costs of the loss of female talent, which are often much higher than male talent. It takes the costs of education and training (the 'investment') on the one side, and the costs of recruitment, selection (such as executive search fees, advertisements, sponsoring of conferences, and so on), and training of a replacement on the other side.

Financial gain

Many studies have concluded that companies with a relatively high share of women in top management outperform their competitors in terms of results and return on investment.[13] In addition, their corporate governance systems are of a better quality. However, none of the studies has actually been able to irrefutably demonstrate a causal relationship between the representation of women at the top level and the business results. This has made many organizations cautious about using these studies in their business case because they may provoke resistance among employees. Despite the fact that the number of female CEOs is very low, even the possible impact of having a female CEO on the company's results has been investigated.[14] The reported results are again positive. The number of similar studies has exploded in the past years, and their results have showed consistency. This has led to serious debates in the boardrooms about a wider variety of topics around diversity. After all, even if a causal relationship cannot be proven, the sheer number of results pointing in the same direction cannot be easily ignored. On the other hand, those that use the studies as the leading argument in their endeavor to increase the number of women on boards may take note of the words of Anne Mulcahy, former CEO of Xerox: 'Women should have an equal chance to fail or succeed. I would not like to see reports indicating that women fail more often than men. The debate should really be about diversity and innovation.'

8   Improved quality of decision-making and corporate governance

In a team made up of people with different backgrounds, education, management styles, age, nationality, gender, and so on, the wide variety in perspectives ensures that a problem will be analyzed more thoroughly and in greater detail. Diversity results in an improvement of corporate governance.[15] Because minority viewpoints and interests are included from the beginning, the final decision will more adequately incorporate those viewpoints than in regular decision-making processes.

Safeguard against group-think

Diversity in teams prevents the widespread phenomenon of 'group-think', a process in which decision-makers try to prevent conflicts occurring and refrain from asking questions, challenging viewpoints, testing new ideas, and evaluating less likely solutions. Group-think occurs when there is a strong cohesion among group members. Questions and ideas that could challenge the social structure and cohesion are not brought to the table. Individual doubts and criticisms are swallowed. Members rationalize information that conflicts with the ideas of the group and frequently 'put away' group members who challenge the group's thinking. Decisions influenced by group-think may be hurried, irrational, and unbalanced. Creative solutions are not taken into account and as a result not all stakeholders feel that their interests have been sufficiently acknowledged in the final decision. The members of the group often feel confident and optimistic, which may well lead to taking irresponsible risks.

Impact of women's presence

Scandinavian research has demonstrated that the presence of women in the boardroom leads to enrichment of information, perspectives, discussion, and decision-making.[16] A well-documented effect is that members prepare better for meetings when women are part of the board. Women are said to ask questions others are reluctant to, and to pose them in a different way than usual. The atmosphere in the boardroom may change as a result. This development diminishes the danger of group-think.

Very recent research into Norwegian firms found that board effectiveness increases with the share of women on the board.[17] Decreased levels of conflict were noted and it was suggested that women's enhanced sensitivity toward others and their interests had a positive impact on the board decision-making processes regarding the company's strategy.

The critical mass debate

It can be questioned in what way women who are the only one on the board can have a substantial impact on the board's way of working. Consensus seems to have developed around the idea that one needs a critical mass (around 30 percent) of women in the boardroom before the advantages of diversity will manifest themselves.[18] Women have reported that as soon as they are part of a group of at least three out of ten, they are no longer considered to be 'a woman' but simply 'a board member'. In this situation the differences between men and women will disappear, and women will be more comfortable contributing their skills and abilities than on boards where they are the only one. Some report that they feel more confident and supported to give their opinion. A recent Danish study showed that the 'one and only' female board member is often seriously influenced by the majority.[19] She is likely to conform to the prevailing opinion in order to be accepted as a competent board member.

Organizations that embrace the benefits diversity can bring to improve the quality of their decision-making processes will therefore appoint women to positions of crucial value to the organization.

9   Driver for innovation and higher productivity

In a number of studies about the impact of cultural diversity on the quality of decision-making,[20] gender diversity is linked to this quality and to innovation. People with different backgrounds bring a variety of ideas and perspectives which strengthen the creativity of the team and its ability to innovate. According to research among MBA students,[21] a higher degree of diversity in the team resulted in higher productivity, with less frequent meetings.

Companies that have defined innovation as one of their core competencies and their diversity policy as an instrument to achieve an innovative culture will position the formal responsibility for diversity and innovation with the *strategic marketing function*.

10   Positive impact on ethical behavior

Although men and women use the same ethical norms in corporations, research shows that women make more ethical choices, especially in 'gray' situations when clear-cut choices are not apparent.[22] Women have higher scores on care for others and truthfulness, whereas men score better on fair play. Women are more inclined to take action when they are in doubt about the ethical implications of a decision. Many whistle-blowers in organizations turn out to be women. These differences in ethical behavior are also influenced by the length and the level of management experience.

How to use the ten perspectives

The ten perspectives above are all being used, separately and in combination with each other, as guidelines to develop a variety of measures to improve the representation of women in decision-making positions. However, statistics show that significant improvements in the representation of women on corporate boards are primarily recorded in the Scandinavian countries, and in particular in Norway with 42 percent due to legislated quotas backed up by serious penalties.

CHAPTER 5

The Power of Frames

Frameworks are the result of the interpretations of our personal experiences and of those we trust. Frames help us navigate through the information around us and enable us to make choices. They provide us with a structure so that we may analyze and categorize the world around us. Frames, however, can have a negative impact on our leadership development when they are based on prejudices and assumptions.

In this chapter we discover how some of our own mental frameworks came into existence and how we can operate effectively in a society built by frames. We also address how to remodel our own limiting frames to more open and transparent structures.

5.1 Origins of our frames

First, it is important to investigate which frames you use daily and how they have developed over the years. A key part of this process involves determining to what extent you have been confronted with people who are different from you in terms of background, gender, religion, ethnicity, culture, age, and so on and in what way this has shaped your judgment and your association with those who are different. Self-reflection is necessary in order to gain insight into the mental frames you have adopted and the manner in which they influence your behavior and activities. The following questions may be helpful in starting the process of discovery:

1. How diverse was your family and the neighborhood you grew up in?

2. What was the composition of your family during your childhood (parents, siblings) and what is the composition of your family now?

3. How diverse were schools, universities, associations, and clubs to which you belonged? What was the choice to join based upon?

4. How diverse is the team you work with in your organization?

5. Have you managed or been managed by someone with a different background to yours?

6. What expectations do you hold of people who are different from you?

7. Have you experienced a situation in which you were a minority? How did you feel?

From mother to manager

The composition of the family in which you were raised has a profound influence on your frames of thinking. Successful women often report that they were stimulated and motivated to excel during their childhood, just like their brothers. The behavior of fathers, especially, is of great importance for daughters when they achieve success in business. Mothers, on the other hand, are reported to have a different impact on the career of a successful daughter.

Serving as an illustration is the story of a successful female executive who found her inspiration in the transformation of her mother when she started to build up her own career, having cared for her daughter and the rest of the family for over 12 years. To the daughter it made an indelible impression that the initially caring and almost invisible mother, who had devoted herself entirely to the well-being of her family, suddenly changed into an adult woman who actively took part in business and social life. Consequently, the relationship of the married couple changed too, as the father had been raised in the traditional manner, in which the wife is subordinate to the husband and, as such, should not have the ambition to develop a large degree of independence of thought. Before the eyes of the 12-year-old daughter, the mother transformed from a dependent, sacrificial mother into a manager with talents and energy. When a daughter becomes aware of the transformation of her mother's life when her mother starts working outside of the home, she can become resentful or it may stimulate her own ambitions.

Champions of diversity

A similar experience is reported by fathers who watch their daughters struggle with challenges in the workplace. These close-to-home experiences often cause a fundamental shift in their mental models. In the outside world we recognize these men as champions of diversity, who actively seek out and develop female talents. The struggles of their daughters inspire them to influence the environment so that their daughters' chances for a successful career will improve.

It is important to become aware of your own history and how it has shaped your mental models. However, new insights and experiences may lead you to make different choices than before, and new mental models may be constructed. The first step in this process is to realize the existence of these frames and the impact they have.

Scarcity creates unfamiliarity

At societal level, frameworks represent the collective knowledge or conscious. How society looks upon women leaders will affect our individual frames.

It is a fact that women are more used to being led by men than vice versa. Especially in large corporations with around 25 percent of women in middle management, and fewer in senior management, it is no surprise that men have limited experience with female managers. Less successful female managers, therefore, may attract disproportionate attention. Some men may have so few experiences or so few positive experiences that they become slightly uncomfortable with having to deal with women in the workplace. Some men may even develop, consciously or unconsciously, some form of resistance. Their lack of positive experiences with female managers may result in less appreciation and even lower expectations of them altogether. Unfortunately, this mental model pervades their behaviors in new situations with female leaders, too. It soon becomes a self-fulfilling prophecy.

Interestingly, the same phenomenon occurs with female employees who have female managers. They can also develop a mental framework, believing that women are less effective leaders due to negative experiences with them. It may also reflect their personal beliefs that they themselves do not possess leadership qualities or simply have not had a chance to discover and recognize them. Consequently, they will be convinced that women are simply not leadership material and all their experiences will support this belief.

These beliefs are defined by the mental models in our society, in which we still rarely encounter successful female leaders who serve as role models for both women and men. Society has lowered its expectations and beliefs around female leaders and has rated them lower than their male counterparts. This collective mental model is severely limiting the development of individual female leadership potential and needs to be addressed at societal level.

'The one and only'

For many women, being 'the one and only' in the management team is not the exception but the rule. Few men have this experience the other way round. An example is a male professor who was used to giving presentations to top management in the corporate world. Because his audiences were primarily businessmen, he dressed like them for the occasion, showing respect for their corporate culture and blending into the group. When giving a presentation to a professional women's group, he entered the room in baggy cotton trousers and a Hawaiian shirt. One of the business women in the audience addressed the issue: 'I have had the pleasure to attend some of your speeches in corporate settings and I noticed that you were always neatly dressed in a business suit. Why did you choose to dress down this time?' The professor realized that his mental model of 'just doing a talk for a group of women' had lowered his expectations of his audience's professionalism and the way he should approach the presentation, in terms of both behavior and dress. He confided that this personal experience of being 'the only one' taught him more about the impact of prejudice than everything he had learned and read about the topic.

5.2 Framing leadership competencies

The common belief that women cannot be competent leaders, whereas in fact they are simply just not visible as such in our society – the female leadership paradox – has made the discussions on how to promote more women to top management increasingly difficult and often based on incorrect premises. The most important example is the current debate about a legislative quota. In many European countries the need to implement a legislative quota for a minimum representation of women in top management has been discussed. One of the most popular arguments against legislation is that it will lead to incompetent women being appointed to boards. Interestingly, in this discussion it is rarely questioned if the current male board members are competent. Male board members are considered to be competent whereas women are considered to be incompetent unless they have proven the opposite. The quota discussion is a reflection of a collective feeling of insecurity: women cannot make it on their own and need a helping hand. Unfortunately, this feeling can be found among men and women alike.

Ambitious and talented women only

Another example is the argumentation used to build activities which stimulate the advancement of women to senior management. Many action groups or corporate activities use the wording 'talented' or 'ambitious' when addressing the target group of women for their activities. Courses for 'ambitious' or 'talented' women are popular. This language contains hidden messages. It expresses a clear difference between women who are talented and ambitious and those who are not. This distinction is never found in courses for men. We seem to take it for granted that either all men are talented or ambitious or the distinction is not really relevant. After all, it is obvious that not all men are talented and motivated to achieve a top position. The additives 'talented' and 'ambitious' for women's courses may even be interpreted as an apology, as if to tell the establishment: 'Don't be afraid because we only want the talented women to be promoted and not the rest of them . . .'. The words can play an unintended, undermining role because they refer to the fact that maybe women themselves also are not convinced of their competencies to be in top positions. These additives create an artificial differentiation and exclusion of large groups of women who do not feel comfortable with this development. Ultimately it will be counterproductive in creating the critical mass needed to bring about structural changes. Solidarity among all women may prove to produce better results.

Diverse or universal?

Another example is the fact that even if women represent half of the world's population and almost half of the workforce, policies for their career advancement are often labeled 'diversity policies'. Statistics prove that women are as universal as men. Diversity policies applied to women therefore reinforce the notion that women are a minority.

5.3 Reframing as a strategy

Mental models can have limiting effects because they prevent other viewpoints being taken into account.[1] Our experiences and our interpretations shape our frames, together with influences from our social context. The ability to reframe our mental models immediately opens up new opportunities and removes barriers in our careers. It is a crucial tool in the professional women's toolkit to reach your goals.

The lure of logic

The beauty and at the same time difficulty of frames and mental models is that they are so familiar and so logical. Nevertheless, it is often easy to discover which prejudices and preconceptions lay behind them. For instance, the term 'gender pay gap'[2] refers to the fact that women on average still receive a lower salary for the same work than men. If the gender pay gap in a certain company or sector amounts to 17 percent, it means that women on average earn 17 percent less than men despite the similarity of experience, background, education, tenure, and so on. The starting point of this measurement is that the salary of a male employee is the norm and the lower earnings of a female employee the deviation.

Reframing the logic

Resisting the lure of this logic and reframing the concept of the gender pay gap leads to surprising perspectives. If we take women's salary as the norm, in the above example men earn 20 percent more than women. Thus, men are in fact overpaid. In our highly segregated labor market, working in typically female professions and sectors (like health care) is less financially rewarding than making a career in typically male professions or sectors (like technical professions). Taking into account this effect, questioning our frames may lead to the new insight that there is actually a 'female gender pay gap' and a 'male gender pay gap'. By reframing the issue, we generate transparency and question our own beliefs. After all, we have become used to the idea that it is women who are being underpaid instead of men being overpaid. Reframing common beliefs like this leads to developing a deeper understanding and, consequently, may prevent feelings of victimization of women in general.

Limiting our leadership competencies

Another example of the impact of frames and their limitations is the female leadership paradox, as discussed in Chapter 4. By linking the more feminine leadership qualities such as empathy, care, and communication skills to the gender of women, and the more masculine traits such as result orientation and strength to men, both genders become framed and thus limited in their behaviors. Since leadership is a male concept in our world, women have difficulty in being recognized and appreciated as credible leaders. Reframing and broadening our conceptual thinking models around leadership will, in the end, produce a different mental model, lifting the limitations stereotypes hold for both genders.

From work–life balance to work–life integration

Reframing can have a profound impact on your personal situation, too. Many women who combine a career with raising children and other care responsibilities (for partner, family, neighborhood, or society) experience feelings of guilt. These are often caused by the assumption that they are not able to carry out all their roles effectively. The norm in society still is that women bear the first responsibility for care tasks. Self-development and self-actualization often take second place. Although generation Y seems to be moving away from this preconception to a more balanced division of household tasks and career ambitions between partners, the traditional mental model is still popular. Young women who are successful in changing their inner beliefs to 'we are partners in raising our children' and 'we share the right to self-development and career development' report that they no longer suffer from feelings of guilt and lead more balanced and happy lives.

Balancing the demands at home and at work presents a well-known dilemma for women, and increasingly for men, too. The eternal balancing act requires poise and continuous efforts to maintain the sensitive equilibrium. Like gymnasts on the balance beam exercising the most difficult movements without losing their grip, work–life balance needs training. No training will prevent accidents from happening. The term 'work–life balance' implies that if you concentrate on work, 'life' might pass you by, and the other way round. Like a see-saw, work–life balance is the point you pass whenever life or work takes over. The impossibility of the situation cuts down the motivation of both women and men. Reframing the issue opens up the possibility to use a different word which creates a natural connection between the two components: work–life integration. The current company structures and the widespread use of technology enable us to combine the work and home life in a more flexible way than ever before. Men and women embrace the possibility to simply get out their laptop, work for another hour, and then take care of their children. Employers understand the importance of this new need for flexible working and move toward reward systems based on output instead of the number of hours in the office.

New mental models needed

By setting out to discover the hidden prejudices in our language, such as those shown above, and reframing the restrictive concepts into positive and constructive ones, we actively shape new mental models for ourselves, which will enable us to move forward, take advantage of the technological progress, and open up unseen new possibilities for our careers and lives.

5.4 FAQs

The first case study in this chapter deals with the conflicting images between the traditional roles of women in general, as 'the wife of', and the modern role of women, as business professionals. The second case study deals with the more traditional role of women in business, as assistant or in supporting roles, and the modern role of women as business professionals. The last case study is to do with the different perceptions of the traditional women's role of caretaker.

- Why am I treated as 'wife of' instead of business professional?
- Why do they address me as secretary or assistant?
- Why is it OK if my partner collects the children from school and not if I do?

Why am I treated as 'wife of' instead of business professional?

Description

The female director of a multinational investment banking company is serving on an expatriate contract in Malaysia. Her husband gave up his job to follow her career move and found a managerial position at a local company. Because she is responsible for the expansion of the company's client base in neighboring countries, one of her most crucial activities is to build up a network of highly valued business contacts. Attending conferences, receptions, and social events is an important source of connections in the Asian business culture.

Unexpectedly she is confronted with traditional cultural behaviors. At receptions and social functions her husband receives questions about his position, whereas she is simply ignored. After a polite nod she is quickly introduced to the other women present. They are trailing spouses and primarily occupy themselves with household issues and voluntary work. Eager to develop business relationships, she leaves the women's group to start a conversation with some of the businessmen. However, they make it very clear that her contribution is not appreciated by them or by their wives, who may perceive her as a threat to their marriage. She is shocked when one of the businessmen asks her rather matter-of-factly: 'So, what do you do all day?'[3] His message is that she is 'the wife of' and should behave as such.

How can she still be successful in her professional role and enjoy working for the company?

Analysis

This case study is an example of reconciling potentially conflicting roles of business professional and 'the wife of'. As a professional, the female director feels annoyed about this situation and the fact that she is not recognized as a professional. It is not uncommon for women in such a situation to start doubting their own behaviors and blaming their own conduct for the reactions they receive. In this case, the situation could have a negative impact on the female director's assignment to expand the company's network of business contacts and, consequently, could even undermine her business success. When she refrains from attending the traditional coffee mornings hosted by the ambassador's wife and resists requests to help working in an orphanage, many expat wives consider her arrogant. She needs to find a good solution to this situation, because not only her professional success but also her social life depends on it.

Strategies

Don't take it personally

The most important strategy is to not take the situation personally. The reactions you receive do not reflect your personality or your attitude toward others. They reflect the expectations people have about the role women in your situation normally have, which is the role of 'the wife of'. Because the reverse situation, a woman as an expatriate manager, does not occur frequently, it is automatically assumed that you are one of the trailing spouses, too. If you don't take it personally, you are better equipped to respond effectively than when you get irritated about the prejudice. Irritated or arrogant responses in these situations will only lead to negative reactions from the other side, since they may feel exposed to their own prejudices.

Use humor as a tool

Try to find humor in the situation. Develop a few witty or hilarious responses which will make you more relaxed and better prepared for similar situations. Humor is a powerful tool to combat prejudices and stereotypes as it often serves as an ice-breaker, especially in situations that are of a more personal nature, such as social events. Instead of giving an irritated answer, you may consider replying to the question 'So, what do you do all day?': 'Thank you for asking. Actually, I am quite busy during the day managing investments worth one billion euros.'

Keep your eye on the business

In order to be able to fulfill your business assignment, the following strategies may be proposed:

- Prepare well for an event or reception by asking for a list of the attendees so you can plan ahead for business conversations with specific guests and organize introductions to people you do not know yet.
- Investigate any possible connections you might have with the host or any guests of honor; in Asian cultures you are as important as the important people you know.
- Take a proactive attitude toward introducing your business relations to others. This increases the chance of them introducing you to theirs.

- Become a member of the expat club or business circle, or accept a board position of a school, university, or institute. This will not only enlarge your network but also promote your reputation as a professional.
- If you want to be seen as a professional, act professionally at all times and refrain as much as possible from activities other professionals would not embark upon.

Why do they address me as secretary or assistant?

Description

A female partner at a consultancy firm operates the photocopier in the hallway whenever her assistant is unavailable. One day she is using the device when it suddenly breaks down. Since this happens regularly she makes an effort to repair the machine herself by removing some of the parts. Someone passes by and asks, 'When you have finished, could you copy this for me? My room is at the end of the hall, room 15. Thanks!'

A similar situation occurs when a female director of the firm visits a potential new client. She takes a male junior consultant with her for coaching on the job. During the conversation the male client only speaks to the junior consultant, acting as if the female director is not present. Even when she addresses the client directly, he automatically directs his answers to the junior consultant.

Analysis

Both situations are classic examples of thinking in frames. Women who operate the photocopying machine or who accompany a male colleague are assumed to be the secretary or assistant. It is clear that a formal position in itself is not sufficient to be taken seriously as a professional. It is important to recognize that the treatment you receive is not caused by you or your behavior, but is exclusively the result of cultural framing. These cases are well known in traditional male-dominated companies in which very few women have reached positions of importance.

Strategies

Use humor

In large organizations it is impossible to know everyone personally, so there is a real risk that similar situations will happen regularly. Interestingly, women in these organizations often make the same mistake and also address their female colleague as assistant or secretary. The prejudices work on both sides and are relatively innocent since they are based on ignorance and misguided expectations. The use of humor often produces the best result, as beside a photocopying machine is hardly the right place to start a serious debate about gender stereotyping. In the first case study it is important to demonstrate that your colleague is wrong in assuming you are a secretary. An example of a witty remark which indicates that there is no difference in formal hierarchy between you is 'Sure. If you get me some coffee then. Cappuccino, one sugar, please. Thanks!'

Prepare your announcement

For important meetings, such as client acquisition meetings, it is advisable to announce the formal hierarchy between you and your colleague well in advance. Either you do this yourself or you have someone else in your company organize your announcement. Make sure that the potential client is aware of your position and qualifications and those of your colleague.

Take the lead

Take time to introduce yourself and emphasize your responsibilities and your colleague's at the start of the meeting. Take the lead in the conversation and actively prevent the answers to your questions from being directed at your colleague. You can prevent this from happening by regular interventions, nodding and through your posture and seating at the table.

This strategy only works when the potential client responds well to it and accepts you as the lead conversation partner. If the client's behavior persists and your colleague continues to act in the same manner, you need to take charge in your relationship with your junior consultant too, by giving him clear directions on his behavior.

Why is it OK if my partner collects the children from school and not if I do?

Description

A high-potential female senior account manager with a direct reporting line to the board is planning to decrease her working hours in order to spend more time with her daughter. The company's employment conditions include the possibility for all employees to temporarily work for four days, nine hours without losing any benefits, such as their lease car or their employer's contribution to the costs of child care. The senior account manager's partner is using the same arrangement under his employer's contract at another company. Her request to make use of this right evokes opposition; management expects it will negatively impact on the service she delivers to her clients. Nevertheless, she pushes through and starts working according to the new arrangement.

In order to prevent problems for her colleagues she remains available by telephone and even attends important meetings five days a week. Her workload stays the same and she continues to work in the evenings and weekends in order to 'compensate', as she feels, for her 'day off'. Her results continue to be in line with what has been agreed to. Spending more time with her daughter, she no longer feels like 'superwoman' and her family also clearly benefits from the new arrangement.

A year later the board informs her that her colleagues say she is no longer committed to her job. Despite keeping up the pace and delivering on her promises she suddenly bears the stamp of 'working part time'. Her rational reasoning that an official 36-hour working week cannot really be considered 'part time' and that she continues to deliver results is not taken seriously. One of the board members puts it into words: 'It is all about perception.'

Women report comparable experiences when they have to collect their children from school. If their spouse collects them, he receives compliments at work for taking his work–life balance so seriously, whereas she is blamed for a lack of professionalism and commitment.

Analysis

Despite the official employment conditions, many women find that (temporarily) reducing their working hours in order to care for children or the elderly calls into question their ambition and commitment to the job. The essence of prejudice is that it is ubiquitous and applicable to all group members. All women who work less, even if it's just a few hours or temporarily, are considered to be less serious about, and less committed to, their job. Even if women in senior positions work part time for a while, they stand a real chance of losing their authority toward their colleagues and staff.

This prejudice is in contrast to the widespread acceptance of male colleagues who work part time for a while, for instance to complete an MBA, give lectures at university, accepting a part-time position as professor or a part-time appointment to a supervisory or non-executive board. Seldom is their dedication and commitment to their job questioned.

Strategies

Make technology your friend

Many women do not realize that reducing their working hours has direct consequences for their pension plan and other labor conditions. The impact of temporary part-time work, therefore, can be much longer than expected in terms of financial independence. Especially for ambitious career-minded women, it may not be the best strategy to cut down on working hours. In corporate cultures with prevailing prejudices like these, the most effective strategy may well be to continue working full time but building into one's agenda more flexibility in hours and including periods of working from home. By making smart use of technology and by planning methodically, you can create more time for family life without consequences for your career or salary. Prerequisites for success in this case are, first, the ability to say 'no' when extra or difficult assignments come your way. Secondly, you need to have a team around you to which you can sufficiently delegate some of the less crucial tasks. Nowadays more and more companies accept flexible working arrangements, provided that the service to clients is not negatively affected. By taking responsibility for organizing a solution yourself, you gain respect from your colleagues and maintain your good reputation as a professional.

Respect your own privacy

A different strategy can be found in the way you communicate. When you have experienced negative reactions to certain behavior, as when you have to leave a meeting early for private reasons, you can announce your departure more strategically. For instance, combine it with a business activity such as visiting a client located in the neighborhood or calling upon a sick employee. It is not necessary to always share all your personal information with everyone. Transparency and openness about personal issues have boundaries in cultures in which it might harm your reputation as a professional.

Choose output-driven organizations

It is easier to organize flexibility around your work schedule in corporations with a culture of managing output and results instead of availability and working hours. Such a culture will enable you to shift some of your business activities to after-office hours, thus creating more flexibility for family activities during the daytime.

CHAPTER 6

Culture

Organizational or corporate culture relates to the way we work, the way we interact with each other, and the way we get things done in an organization. Our professional success largely depends on our ability to understand different organizational cultures and to apply methods to operate effectively within their parameters. If you are missing the ability or ambition to adjust to a specific culture, your results may lag behind and you may start to feel undervalued and underappreciated as a consequence.

In this chapter you will use the Inclusive Leadership quadrants as a tool to investigate the behavioral aspects of the culture you are currently working in. This exercise serves to deepen your understanding of the characteristics and the strategies that create success or failure.

6.1 Quadrants of culture

The Centre for Inclusive Leadership has developed a model, shown in Figure 6.1, which provides insight into the relationship between the perceived value of diversity, in the broadest sense of the word, and the ability of an organization to adapt.[1] This model can also be used to gain knowledge about the important characteristics of the culture of the organization you are operating in. It will enable you to develop more effective approaches to situations which might be more frequently experienced in such a culture.

The basic assumption of the Inclusive Leadership model is that all differences (in culture, background, experience, gender, religion, and so on) are acknowledged and appreciated. The differences are complementary to one another and ensure that a wide variety of perspectives is taken into account. Deviations from standard patterns of thinking and logic are actively sought and embraced to further improve the quality of the decision-making process.

The x-axis of the model records the *perceived value of the difference*. At zero (the far left end), the perceived value is zero, gradually increasing toward the other end of the x-axis (to the far right) until its maximum. Because everyone has a unique view on the importance of diversity, the value we attach to it also varies from person to person. Women experience

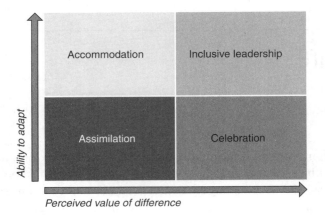

Figure 6.1 Quadrants of culture

standing out as a result of being the minority in a team significantly differently than men do. The reality for women in those circumstances is not the same as for men in similar circumstances. This can also be observed at the organizational level. In many companies in which gender diversity is proclaimed to be a crucial part of the human resources strategy, reality is different when analyzing the numbers. Female employees may even report negative experiences despite the policy.

The y-axis of the model reflects the *organization's ability to adapt.* It indicates to what extent the organizational culture recognizes differences and captures their value in order to become more effective, more innovative, and more distinguishing toward competitors. Organizations positioned at the zero point are not equipped to recognize differences; the value of the difference is zero to them. Organizations at the high end of the y-axis, on the other hand, have developed the competency to effectively adapt to the variety of viewpoints diversity brings.

When we apply the above concept to the experiences of women being labeled 'diversity' in organizations, four main corporate cultures can be distinguished.

The Assimilation Quadrant

When the perception of the value of the differences and the adaptability of the organizational culture meet at point zero, the company's culture is characterized by a high degree of assimilation. Managers actively, or even forcefully, promote the company's values and goals to their employees and ignore any other perspectives. Differences are disparaged, ignored, or replaced by unambiguous viewpoints of management. Managers are convinced that they are the only ones who know what is best for the company. Often, there is a strong social cohesion between employees with a focus on procedures and policies. Consistency and coherence prevail, and individual deviations are disposed of as non-constructive. Employees who develop themselves in another direction than management desires run the risk of being labeled 'annoying'. The well-known saying applies: *'My way or the high way.'* Management does not pursue the realization of competitive advantages of having a diverse workforce.

The relative advantage of an assimilation culture is that it creates a relatively homogenous environment in which differences of opinion and conflicts are limited. Discrimination rarely takes place because dissidents either completely adapt to the culture or leave the organization altogether. Manuals and procedures ensure a high degree of consistency in policy. The company is able to take and implement decisions relatively quickly because the strong cohesion between employees dictates their actions.

An obvious disadvantage of an assimilation culture is that the company may have difficulty remaining successful in fast-changing environments. The competency to solve problems creatively, to develop new markets, and to produce new products will be limited due to the absence of diversity. The proverb applies: *'When all think alike, no one is thinking very much.'* The absence of resources and mental models to formulate quick responses to competitors' strategies and actions makes the company less successful in dynamic markets.

The Accommodation Quadrant

As soon as the company starts to acknowledge the value of differences as a factor in the corporate culture, and its ability to adapt to changing circumstances improves, it moves toward the Quadrant of Accommodation. Employees, who are different with regard to their background or behavior, gender or otherwise, are recognized and their inclusion is considered to present a moral obligation (human rights) or business issue (customer target group). Policies and facilities that address the requirements of these special employee groups are developed. An example is the so-called *mommy track* for women who want to work fewer hours for a specific period of time in order to raise their children or care for an elderly relative. In a corporate culture of Accommodation, employees who differ from the norm are considered 'special needs' for which the company has to develop extra

arrangements. They are clearly set apart from the mainstream of the organization. Management considers the special arrangements as 'extras' or
palliatives which are the first ones to be discontinued when business results
deteriorate and costs need to be cut. The potential positive value of diversity does not permeate the culture of decision-making but is halted at the
working conditions and facilities. Management makes an effort to respect
employees' different backgrounds and viewpoints but struggles to integrate
the differences at the various levels. Consequently, the integration of differences does not lead to the development of a new corporate culture but only
to superficial outside changes.

The strategy to develop specific policies for special target groups of
employees could result in an incoherent management style. Women may
be treated differently than men. Both groups are likely to develop resistance against preferential treatments, which undermines the social cohesion
and puts pressure on the corporate culture. Victimization and discrimination
may occur.

The Quadrant of Celebration

When differences are exaggerated and disproportionally valued, the
corporate culture gradually moves to the Quadrant of Celebration. If we
apply this to gender differences, the quadrant could be named The
Female Advantage Quadrant. Management is convinced that all women
are empathic and trustworthy and have excellent communication, social,
and people-management skills. These specific feminine leadership qualities are considered important for the success of the business. Consequently,
women are primarily appointed to positions that call on their feminine qualities, such as human resources management, public relations, education
and training, communication, facilities management, and other supporting roles. Very few women serve in line-management positions in the
heart of the business, such as business unit manager, or other functions
with bottom-line responsibility or of crucial strategic importance. In many
cases the top levels of the supporting functions are populated by men
again. Often, the human resources director of a large company is a man,
whereas his management team and staff consist of more than 70 percent
women.

Organizations that operate in the Quadrant of Celebration typecast
women for specific roles according to the male concept of leadership,
which we discussed in Chapter 4. The stereotypes resulting from this thinking are often more difficult to oppose than open discrimination because
they are based on a positive evaluation of feminine qualities. Management

is unaware of the limiting effect of this aspect of the corporate culture on the talents of all women in the organization. Women with all-round leadership qualities and the ambition to fulfill positions as line manager, business unit manager, or CEO often leave the organization after they have declined a number of positions characterized as 'women's functions' or supporting roles.

The Inclusive Leadership Quadrant

When the perceived value of the differences is high, as well as the adaptability of the organization, the corporate culture is moving toward an inclusive culture. In this case the differences in values and background are actively managed and employees are encouraged to discover them. Open discussions are promoted and 'lobbying' behaviors discouraged. 'Transparency' is the key word in an inclusive culture. Management creates a climate of trust and openness which stimulates employees to integrate their own views with others. Next to a thorough understanding of other people's viewpoints, experiencing the impact is actively promoted. Management publicly emphasizes the importance of diversity and walks the talk by acting accordingly. The inclusive leadership style is flexible and adaptable to any given situation without abandoning its underlying principles.

The work environment is deliberately structured in such a way that personal interaction and frequent communication is the key to optimal fulfillment of an employee's tasks. The organizational goals are created jointly within the team. In many cases, the remuneration system is wholly or partially based on achieving the team or group goals. The reward system is based on transparency and fairness. Rules and procedures play a supporting more than a restrictive role and can be adapted if they work against the culture.

The overall goal is to develop a richer and more complex organizational culture that embraces change and stimulates learning. Management's primary role is to be a facilitator in the process of developing an inclusive culture.

The core of inclusive leadership resonates in the saying: '*What we shouldn't do is say "they" should be more like us. We should create a* **new us.**'

The above descriptions of managerial behavior and characteristics of corporate culture in four specific models of corporate culture can help you to assess in which quadrant your own organization or unit operates. Different cultures or a mix of the four basic models can be found in one company.

6.2 Copying is a choice

Culture is the collective noun for the use of specific language and habits that are shared and accepted among a group of people. In order to operate effectively in a certain culture we need to understand and speak the language, and adopt the habits. In a work environment the desire to achieve your goals may force you to copy certain language or behaviors of the prevailing group culture. Especially in organizations operating in the Assimilation and Accommodation Quadrants, you can feel pressured to accept or display certain types of leadership behaviors that are contrary to your own beliefs. This can seriously compromise your feeling of authenticity as a leader.

Power talk

Illustrative of power talk in assimilation cultures is the way in which arguments are being used to gain acceptance of an important proposal. In some organizations, employees even threaten to resign if their proposal is rejected. The threat usually does not materialize but the pressure is used to push through a decision. Often, women consider this behavior as dishonest and violating authenticity, especially since most of them would never seriously consider leaving the organization over such an issue. Although this applies to many men too, they are often more inclined to play along, knowing that it will never go that far in the first place. In workshops it has been observed that women often rely on using rational arguments to influence the decision-making process in their favor. Unfortunately, this strategy does not always produce the desired result in corporate cultures with strong cohesion between the employees. Despite the qualitative merit of their proposal, it may not get accepted in such a culture.

Proposals should be accepted based on their inherent quality, so the strategy of using reason, which women embark upon, should indeed produce the best results. However, in companies with a strong assimilation or accommodation culture, the chosen strategy may not be rewarded because it violates the unwritten rules of 'how we do things around here'.

Women often place more importance on power talk than is necessary. Over time this may well lead to a feeling of 'banging one's head against the wall' or 'it is lost labor'. In fact, these feelings are the result of a mismatch between specific characteristics of the assimilation culture and the strategies chosen to operate effectively in this environment.

The most effective strategy in these cases is to copy some assimilation behaviors but on your own conditions and within your own parameters of acceptability. Publicly opposing the prevailing culture is a dead-end street, unless structural abuses force you to become a whistle-blower. The written and unwritten rules in assimilation cultures are often so strong that many women abandon their efforts to change the culture and leave the company.

Authenticity under pressure

Authentic leaders know who they are, and what they believe and value. They act upon those values and beliefs, and communicate transparently towards their followers. Being an authentic leader is not 'being yourself always' but representing common values of a community. Research shows that women leaders have more difficulty being recognized by their subordinates as authentic leaders than men.[2]

It is an individual choice in how far you are willing to adapt to a prevailing culture or to move to another company that seems to have a culture which might be more suited to your needs. If you compare working in different corporate environments with an expatriation to a foreign country, a number of similarities surface. Living abroad, we normally do not expect people to adjust to our culture but we put in great effort to learn the rules and habits of our new environment. Even unpleasant behaviors meet with our approval as 'they are all part of the local way of doing things'. The same flexibility in thinking will help us when we temporarily operate in an alien environment, such as management consultants working temporarily in different organizations. As long as we are able to adapt our behaviors and at the same time maintain our personal values and integrity, we will function well in different environments. As soon as we are challenged to act in a way that is foreign to our nature, our integrity and authenticity come under pressure.

How to deal with job demands that violate your sense of authenticity has become a very popular topic among women in the business world. The vanishing act of women on their way to the top is closely related to this question. Research shows that women leave companies with strong assimilation cultures because they feel undervalued and under-challenged. In addition, the much-discussed 'being able to stay yourself' in senior positions is related to this issue.

Values versus behaviors

The dilemmas we experience between our sense of integrity and the demands in the workplace can be reconciled by making a clear distinction between our values on the one hand and our behaviors on the other hand.

Through this split we create space in our behavioral repertoire to respond adequately and flexibly. It also enables us to better understand the behaviors of others toward us since we preclude taking them as direct attacks on our values and integrity. By reducing the differences between cultures, but also between men and women, to the level of chosen behaviors and not of personal values and integrity, we defuse the sensitivity of the discussion. This enables us to not take everything too personally and to approach behavioral differences as procedural and rational. Then we can experiment with various behavioral styles without feeling compromised or violating our integrity. A good leader has a toolkit of effective behaviors in a variety of different cultures and circumstances at his or her disposal.

Practical example

The above principle can be applied to the essential management quality of giving constructive feedback to underperforming employees. It is logical that specific cultural settings require different behaviors to carry out this task successfully.

In formal, bureaucratic, and assimilation cultures our toolkit needs to contain other behavioral styles than those in more informal and inclusive cultures, in which joint responsibility for results dominate. In the first instance the feedback session will be announced formally and will be conducted in the presence of a human resources director. The tone of the conversation will be serious and formal, and the focus will lie on the mistakes and faults of the employee and a plan to improve. Minutes of the feedback session will be inserted in the employee's personnel file.

In a more inclusive corporate culture, or one in which collective responsibilities and team results are the norm, the team leader will address the underperformance of the employee in a team meeting at first. The primary goal will be to understand why the employee is deviating from the jointly agreed norms and violating common values. After that, the team will discuss how the employee's performance can be brought back to normal standards and what assistance the team members can give in the process.

Effective behavior toolkit

It is clear that a team leader in two different cultures needs tailor-made approaches (addressing the individual versus the team), different words (using formal versus informal conversation), and tone (expressing seriousness versus displaying empathy) to convey the same message effectively. An effective leader understands the necessity to develop a toolkit of behaviors to be effective in every situation. A prerequisite, however, is to stay loyal to and rooted in your own values.

Acquiring a broad behavioral repertoire to survive in alien cultures is a necessary skill for women with the ambition to achieve a top position. As the interesting positions become scarcer and competition increases on the way to the top, it may be necessary to use certain behaviors that violate our own image of an ideal leader. However, this *effective behavior toolkit* is one of the most crucial factors for a successful career.

6.3 FAQs

The skill of handling resistance is part of the toolkit of skills for leaders. Resistance comes in many different forms and needs handling in different ways. The following case study describes a situation that is commonly experienced by women who advocate against the underrepresentation of women in senior positions. After the analysis of the case study, a schedule is presented containing various responses to frequently heard arguments in this debate.

How do I manage cultural resistance?

Description

A female director is introduced to one of the most powerful board members, who is a prominent part of the 'old boys' network'. At one point in the conversation the absence of women at top levels of corporations comes up. The board member responds positively by saying that 'this topic is right up my alley'. Encouraged by his enthusiasm, the female director inquires after his concrete activities to promote women to top positions. Without answering her question directly, he states that there is really no problem at all since there are many women CEOs of Fortune 500 companies, for instance Indra Nooyi of PepsiCo and Ursula Burns at Xerox. To her response that only 15 out of 500 companies (3 percent) are led by a woman,[3] and that this holds true for most developed countries, so there surely must be a problem, the board member expresses his views: 'Women in most European countries and the United States are lucky because they don't have to pursue a career, which women in, for instance, Norway or Sweden are obliged to do due to social pressure.' The female director's arguments that the ageing population requires the use of all talents at all levels, including women, that diversity leads to improved quality of decision-making, and that companies need to take their role in society seriously and cannot afford to leave half of the population outside were not met with enthusiasm. The conversation simply ended.

Analysis

There are many forms of resistance regarding the topic of women's career advancement. In the many workshops I have conducted in companies with severely low levels of women in top management, the most popular ones were:

- 'If you really want to have a career, you don't have a problem at all in our company.'
- 'There is nothing wrong with our corporate culture, but we just don't have any qualified women.'
- 'Women leave or don't pursue a career for family reasons.'
- 'Women are simply not part of our culture; we just like to talk about fast cars and golf a lot.'
- 'Women who leave work early because of their care for children are simply not so committed.'
- 'I am reluctant to appoint a woman to the team because it changes the atmosphere.'
- 'We don't have women in top positions because we are simply not hiring anyone at the moment.'
- 'Why should we focus on women? It is positive discrimination!'
- 'Why should we bother at all?'
- 'Diversity is flavor of the month.'
- 'It just does not work in our company.'
- 'We want to appoint women but we cannot find them.'
- 'We don't have a problem.'
- 'Women don't want to be promoted.'
- 'Women lack ambition.'

Strategies

In order to respond well to statements like these, good preparation is necessary. Table 6.1 can assist you in formulating possible replies.

The *first column* contains real quotes, so what is actually being said.

In the *second column* you will find a description of what is being done, the facts. In these cases, companies have no or few women in their top teams.

The *third column* analyzes the difference between the two previous ones and describes the origin and form of resistance.

In the *fourth column* you will find suggestions for possible interventions.

Quote	Facts	Type of resistance	Strategic interventions
'Women who have children should stay at home'	*No women in the team*	Personal beliefs (religion, values) Prejudices about the role of women Dogmatic Rigid	**Acknowledge and respect personal beliefs** **Apply the 80/20 rule**[4] **Rely on the group process for corrective behavior**
'I am all for appointing women but my colleagues or clients object'	*No women in the team*	Indirect statement about own values and norms Use of other people's values and beliefs Deflecting and evasive	**Strengthen the knowledge about positive impact (business case)** **Provide tools and support**
'Women add value to the team'	*Few or no women in the team, possibly only in supporting roles*	Political correctness Lip service Conformist	**Challenge to make it happen** **Provide measuring tools**
'. . .' (silence, no statement at all)	*Few or no women in the team*	Evasive Anxiety Uncomfortable	**Raise interest** **Strengthen knowledge about positive impact** **Provide tools and support**

TABLE 6.1 Manifestations of resistance and possible strategic interventions

It is of great importance while dealing with resistance around this topic to realize that most quotes are not meant to be personal attacks but are a reflection of frames and assumptions, as we discussed in Chapter 5. Reacting emotionally or showing irritation will show that you take the statement personally, which seldom leads to dialogue and respectful discussion.

CHAPTER 7

Power and Politics

Power is an integral part of our society and the organizations operating in it. The word 'power' is indissolubly connected to the concept of leadership. Power can be defined as having influence or right of say over others, over valuable resources (financial and human) or over certain decisions. The word 'power' often evokes negative associations when it is equated with authoritative behavior, abuse, and other negative processes in organizations, for instance pushing through controversial decisions and bullying. The ability to build and use a power base is one of the most important competencies in leadership development for women. Overcoming the initial resistance and even accepting the exercise of power as an essential tool of a leader requires increased awareness and specific training during the career.

7.1 The right to power

Literature shows that women, in general, have more referent power than men, based on building personal relationships and being liked.[1] Men more often have legitimate formal power, based on the right of say over others. This right is dependent on formal position and status, but also on an innate conviction of the 'right' to power like a natural right. Men, in general, feel more entitled to power than women. In addition, men concentrate on building 'expert power', based on their competencies and results on the one hand and society's perception of being competent on the other hand. It is fair to say that in general women and men have different points of departure for acquiring and using power in organizations.

7.2 Sources of power

Formal power

There are several sources of power in organizations. The most well known is undoubtedly formal power, which is the power attributed to a person because of his or her formal position. The power belongs to the position and not to the person as an individual. The authorization to sign for approval for certain costs or expenses (limited in currency and time period, for instance) is a public display of power. Organizations are built on hierarchies, in which every layer exercises a certain degree of power, ultimately leading up to the board, which has the most extensive powers. Shareholders are authorized to approve and adopt the company's annual accounts and in many listed companies the non-executive board has the power to put forward a new CEO for appointment by the shareholders. This system of legal rules as part of corporate governance not only regulates the decision-making processes, but also legitimizes its outcomes. The system prevents abuse of power and opens up the possibility for stakeholders to ask a judicial decision if necessary.

Power over scarce resources

Another form of power, which is not necessarily derived from a hierarchical position, is the right to dispose of scarce resources. In this connection, an employee with specialist knowledge on a topic or a unique quality that is not easily replaceable can be seen as a scarce resource. Also, employees with large networks of influential contacts outside the organization may well represent an invaluable and scarce resource to the business. Their position can actually be even more powerful than the formal hierarchical position of their hierarchical manager, which may challenge their formal relationship.

Budgetary power

Related to the scarcity of funds in organizations, employees who have control over budgetary spending can exercise considerable power. Budget responsibility can be fairly limited to small expenses, for instance flowers for sick employees or the costs of a personnel outing. But a budget holder can also be responsible for the purchase of a critically important piece of software to streamline the logistical flow in the organization, worth several millions of euros. Often, budgetary power is connected to a hierarchical position or through escalating models directly derived from the top level of the company. Abuse of power occurs, for instance, when the budget holder for the acquisition of new software decides to accept bribes or certain other services that are not related to the business (such as reimbursement of private travel expenses, or all-inclusive expensive trips to sports events) in the software selection process. Budget holders may well have more influence on decisions through their informal networks than their formal rank would suggest. A relatively low-ranking employee may well have more say in certain decisions than some of the hierarchically higher placed managers.

Budgetary responsibilities are often linked to the responsibility for turnover, sales, or results of the company. The management support organization typically has limited budgets as its expenses are not directly related to the bottom-line results of the company; they are therefore seen as 'overheads' or costs. Senior executives in supporting or advisory roles may well have a lower expense account than their counterparts in the business or even lower-ranking employees in the commercial part of the company. It has been regularly observed that in times of crisis and cost-cutting the budgets of overhead departments are hit hardest, as well as their staff salaries and expenses.

Power of symbols

Another form of power, which has more to do with perception than with reality, is related to the symbols in an organization. A well-known example is the symbolic power of an office. Not only the location, but also the size, the number of windows, the level at which it is located, the entrance, and the distance to facilities may convey a message of power. In many companies 'getting the corner office' equates with being the most valued employee. Depending on the company's culture, the office reflects someone's status and importance within the organization. Other similar symbols are the make and price of a lease car, the newest technological gadgets for phones and computers, but also memberships of prestigious clubs and invitations to important meetings and social events.

Some women have difficulty relating to these status symbols and feel uncomfortable or even impatient. A frequently heard complaint is that in a company's internal moving procedures, too much time is invested in meetings around the details of the move, the selection and allocation of offices, and their layout. Many versions of the new layout of the floor are drafted before a final decision is taken. The process often turns into a political game with power play. Many women are reluctant to actively take part in these types of processes; they rather continue to concentrate on their own tasks, saying 'they don't have time for it'. It can be observed that they adopt a similar approach to prestigious invitations to clubs and events. Since these activities primarily take place after office hours, women often dismiss them as having little to do with their professional careers. In corporate cultures in which status symbols are important, failing to participate in the company's rituals, including visiting these events, may result in not integrating into the informal networks necessary to stay informed. In addition, publicly scorning these practices and symbolisms may be interpreted as arrogance or lack of empathy for what colleagues consider worthwhile.

Informal power

Next to the formal hierarchy, the informal structure is an important source of power. The influence of informal networks depends on a country's culture, local or regional habits (urban versus rural areas), and the company's culture and the culture of the business sector it operates in. Some industries are more politicized than others. Highly politicized companies, such as those operating in the financial services industry, rely strongly on informal connections. The danger of a strong informal culture is that innovative ideas and solutions may not be realized due to fierce resistance in the informal structure blocking the formal hierarchy. The saying 'It is not the proposal itself, but the person who puts it forward' is an expression of a destructive informal culture in which proposals are not evaluated on their content or merit anymore. Eventually, such an informal culture will erode a company from within because talented employees will not feel valued and will choose to move to companies with less restrictive and more open cultures. In the end the company will be left with a group of average employees with strong informal networks, who may not be sufficiently capable of creating new products and developing new markets and thus who seriously compromise the company's long-term existence.

Unwritten rules

Organizations with a strong informal culture have many implicit codes and rules that employees need to abide by, like the above-mentioned example of who is allowed to put forward a proposal to the detriment of it not even being discussed despite its merit. Another popular unwritten rule is the order in which people at a meeting speak. It may not be the 'done thing' to speak up before your manager or more senior executives have spoken. In some organizations the implicit rules are even more restrictive for women. Even if they hold senior or leadership positions, they may be expected to only speak after their male colleagues, sometimes including the junior ones. Senior women who take charge in a meeting are often criticized for being 'too aggressive and not so nice'. One of the most frequently asked questions from women in middle and senior management positions is how to establish their authority without receiving the label of 'not so nice'.

Typical positions with a potential large degree of informal power are secretaries of the board, who prepare, attend, and report on board meetings. The information exchanged during the board meetings is of crucial importance to many employees. However, the secretary cannot make free use of this information as it is of a confidential nature, unless he or she is instructed to communicate about it. Nevertheless, the secretary is very influential because it is common knowledge that he or she is a confidant of the board and can subtly influence certain processes in the company. Special project leaders in charge of strategic initiatives, chairs or secretaries of labor councils or employees' resource groups can hold similar informal influencing power. Last, but not least, former senior executives who have been allocated the honorary title of 'advisor' often exercise substantial power behind the official scenes. Because they are not part of the formal hierarchy they are difficult to approach. In some companies, advisors are being used to mediate in difficult conflicts in which loss of face of top management plays an important role.

Invisible bank account

One of the characteristics of strong informal networks is that the core group is relatively small and has connections across all the different parts of the organization. Often, members have shared significant events and experiences that have created a special bond. It is not uncommon for members to help each other when one of them is suffering from bad results or personal setbacks. Like an invisible bank account, group members support each other through difficulties. Sometimes, group members possess personal or business information of a sensitive nature about each other. After-office-hours drinking parties may result in unhealthy bonds between group members. The power of these informal networks can seriously disrupt objective recruitment and selection processes at the highest level of the organization, leading to the appointment or promotion of less competent but extremely well-connected executives.

The 'old boys' network'

The most well-known example of informal networks and power is the 'old boys' network'. An informal culture can be very effective to a certain extent. It enables processes to be executed efficiently and it serves as the glue in the organization. This has been one of the positive aspects of the so-called 'old boys' network' in many industries in our developed world. The 'old boys' network' consists of an unknown and informal group of top executives of large companies that know each other well and keep each other informed of important developments and threats. Investors and banks have relied on the stability and tranquility these networks have provided in the past and have rewarded companies that were part of this structure. However, the 'old boys' network' can also have a negative effect when new ideas from new generations of managers get blocked and young talents discouraged. This negative impact has become the main public argument to oppose the existence of the 'old boys' network'. The call for transparency and improvement of corporate governance systems has led to board members becoming reluctant to continue serving on some boards. In addition, the corporate governance codes across Europe, of which some have been included in national legislation already, will lead to a further breakdown of the influence of the former 'old boys' networks'.

Characteristics

The workings of this informal network are based on a set of unwritten rules of behavior toward each other and a basic willingness to cooperate and support each other. Trust and confidentiality form the fabric connecting the members. Members have a solid confidence in each other's capacities based on experiences built up over many years. They share the conviction that cooperation will be constructive and conflicts will be kept to a minimum. This does not include uncritical or blind trust, but a basic conviction that one can rely on each other to even settle fundamental differences of opinion and at the same time always maintain a united front to the outside world. Sensitive information is spread subtly and treated confidentially. Disrupting the unity and violating the rules of confidentiality may result in the breakdown of the trust. Especially at top levels in organizations, this may have an effect beyond a particular company or sector and can seriously undermine one's credibility to fulfill a position of trust.

Power over information

Another way to exercise power is related to controlling information. Intentionally keeping back important information from someone is often personally or politically driven. An example of this behavior is a disgruntled consultant who forgets to inform his or her manager that a client wants to be called back immediately because of an urgent issue. Of course, the consultant will face severe penalties if his or her actions become known, but the damage to the manager's reputation and client relationship may have occurred already.

Controlling information takes place at all levels of an organization and involves various sorts of data. Very powerful are those who have informal structures outside the regular information channels that provide them with sensitive and crucial information others do not have access to. If you hear through the grapevine that an important reorganization will be announced in a few months' time which will cause you to lose your job, you can develop a strategy to save your own career. For instance, you can put in a timely request to be relocated to another department or position yourself for a role in the working group that will supervise the implementation of the reorganization. This will enable you to exercise influence on the decision-making process and protect your own interest at the most strategic place. The access to strategic information and its resulting power is a function of the above-mentioned informal networks in organizations.

Power over technology

In some organizations people who are in charge of technology exercise a large degree of informal power. For instance, an employee who is responsible for recording sales commission bookings and is authorized to correct false bookings can have a large amount of informal power over sales account managers. He or she may receive pressure from the sales force to record bookings in their favor in case the rules are not clear and gray areas exist. The difference in education and the experience of the sales managers can make it difficult for the often lower-educated employee to resist the pressures from well-trained sales managers. Furthermore, the absence of automatic safeguards in the system, so individuals cannot tamper with it, and the absence of the so-called four-eyes principle can lead to an undesirable concentration of power with one person.

A similar example can be found in organizations whose IT systems are outdated, manuals absent, and only very few employees that were involved in its development are still around. Their relatively high degree of power is linked to their rare control over certain technology.

7.3 The power paradox

Can power be fun? Are we entitled to like it? Are women really better in 'empathizing with people' and therefore less interested in political games? Or do prejudices prevail and hinder women?

Many women report not being comfortable with exercising power in the traditional sense because they associate it with concepts like 'power structures, power brokers, abuse of power, and power play'. They feel it takes attention away from the content of the job and may jeopardize respectful interaction with colleagues. Another frequently cited reason is that power is connected to violence, like in wars, but also on a smaller, more personal, scale in organizations in the form of social exclusion, intimidation, harassment, and defamation of character.

Perceptions of power

Gender differences in exercising power are deeply rooted in psychological patterns in our childhood. Boys at an early age develop a sense of hierarchy in their group through play and games, based on certain knowledge, intelligence, an ability (e.g. sports), or a specific characteristic (e.g. family reputation). The group hierarchy determines which boy is the informal leader and initiates activity in the group. With girls, a different development takes place, in which personal connections and developing social interpersonal skills are most important. In many girls' groups 'to be nice and to be liked' appears to be the name of the game. The resulting social pressure may prevent girls with above-average intelligence from showing it since it may lead to repercussions from their inner circle. Young girls who display a level of confidence and skills are quickly called too smart, willful, bossy, or not so nice. For boys, intellectual achievements are not seen as a disqualification but as a prerequisite to obtain a higher rank in the informal hierarchy. The implicit hierarchy is causing the strategic behavior of the members toward the group leader. If the leader is successful, this will reflect on all group members, who will support him and remain loyal till the last. This group behavior is characterized by a large degree of solidarity. In girls' groups different norms prevail. Solidarity can be strong but also disappear quickly for apparent simple reasons.

Girls can make up arrears in group behavior partially during their school years. Nevertheless, the gender differences may continue well into adulthood and may be one of the main reasons why women feel uncomfortable with power, formal hierarchy, political games, and certain expressions of solidarity, such as the sometimes seemingly unfounded support and loyalty men in the inner circle provide to each other. Women are known to expel women who do not behave according to their norms, even if they are successful and, sometimes, even because they are successful. Men display more opportunistic behaviors and will continue to support an underperforming leader for a while because of the potential benefits to them.

Powerless but influential

Women manifest themselves in organizations often as influencers behind the scenes instead of power brokers in public. Their role as influencer is not always recognized or valued as it takes place more subtly and covertly. If their informal power becomes evident, it may lead to criticism that they did not play according to the rules. Unfamiliarity with the rules of the game leads to unpredictability and insecurity about their behaviors from the side of the men who have operated so successfully in this structure. Top positions carry risks, like accountability for financial results, but also risks for your personal reputation. Women who display real or perceived unpredictable behavior will be evaluated as posing an extra risk by men and will consequently not be invited to join the team.

Reasons to strive for power

In the end power is simply a means toward achieving an end. Many women feel resistance toward power in its purest form but do want to influence decision-making processes. However, to be heard begins with speaking up and playing the game. During workshops it was frequently observed that as soon as women understood the impact power can have, if used properly and ethically, their resistance against the phenomenon disappeared. A good leader understands that the exercise of power in public is an important tool to realize his or her ambitions but prevents power from taking over and becoming the leader in the process. The ability to use power in the right way and at the right moment is a leadership quality all leaders need to be able to effectively operate. If we define power as 'having the right to make decisions' many reasons can be brought forward why women should aspire to power:

- *Creating a pleasant working environment*
  A formal management position enables you to develop a corporate culture around you that you find stimulating and rewarding. As leader, you set the example and demonstrate in your behavior and communication how you like your employees to interact with each other and their surroundings. By this, you create a climate in which employees can perform to the best of their abilities, in a stable and pleasant environment, with clarity around ethical behavior toward each other.

- *Developing talent*
  One of the most important tasks of a manager is to support employees in developing their talents and skills. Personal coaching, specific training, and exemplary behavior are means to discharge of this task. As a manager you decide which means you will offer to which employee and, as such, you play a significant role in his or her personal development.

- *Driving fundamental change*
  Structural changes in organizations need leadership at the top level and support at the work-floor level. A common cause for disappointments is that you have a vision regarding the necessary transformation of the organization, but you do not have the resources and power to realize it. A position at the sidelines without the formal decision-making responsibility to implement your vision may lead to frustration, burnout, and even resignation. Women, who proclaim not having the ambition to lead, may well experience physical and emotional drain because of the 'injustice' done; their powerlessness may even cause them to leave. Fighting for a promotion or management position might be a better remedy.

- *Building self-confidence as a leader*
  When you exercise formal power, you will receive recognition and appreciation for your achievements. This builds your confidence as a leader. Management positions offer, next to salary, extra benefits as responsibilities increase. Being rewarded for your achievements gives a sense of success and confidence because it takes lots of effort to receive and exercise power.

It starts with ambition

Power and ambition are closely connected. Without power it is impossible to realize your ambitions and without ambition power becomes meaningless. Becoming aware of the need to use power as a resource is an essential part of leadership training for women. They need to start feeling comfortable with recognizing and exercising power, and operating in an environment in which power and the rules of the game are inextricably connected to their responsibilities as manager and leader.

Ambivalence

Women in senior management positions may respond with ambivalence to their formal powers.[2] On the one hand, they are proud of their achievements so far and use their authority to give direction to decision-making processes and exercise supervision over others with the same pleasure and dedication as their male peers. On the other hand, they may experience social pressures to maintain their friendliness and establish harmonious relationships. Striving for competency and control is often considered to be contradictory to striving for balanced relationships and conflict avoidance. Women in senior management positions sometimes struggle with this ambivalence, which is primarily caused by the social expectations in the outside world.

Illustrative of this struggle are the answers some top women give if publicly, at a conference or in a magazine interview, asked: 'How did you reach a top position as the first or only woman at the top level?' Out of modesty many praise their company for giving them the opportunity to develop themselves, and their surroundings for the support they have received. Very few top women start out by saying that they had the competencies to reach a top position, that they had a strategy to get it, and that they worked extremely hard to succeed. Even if they advise aspiring top women that it takes just a lot of very hard work, this often does not sound like a positive encouragement, but more like an excuse for something that is highly exceptional and irregular – especially in careers involving lots of international travel and even relocation of the family to other countries. Unfortunately, ambition, power, and career strategies still seem to carry a negative connotation when it comes to women in our society.

7.4 FAQs

Women may perceive power and politics differently than men. This has a significant impact on their willingness to be promoted to leadership positions. At the organizational level it is one of the most important reasons why women are under-represented at top levels. As expected, many FAQs relate to the topics of power and politics.

- Why is someone else proposing my idea?
- Why do they ask me to deliver bad news?
- Why do I suffer personal attacks?
- Why do I lose my job in the reorganization?
- Why do I miss out on the most favored positions?

Since the first FAQ is by far the most common and the most disruptive according to many women, three small case studies have been developed to address the different aspects of this issue.

Communication forms the blood flow of an organization. It is the instrument through which business is done. Effective communication not only involves the words spoken, but also the tone of voice, the setting, and the persons who are the speaker and the receiver. With this we enter the playground of power and politics.

Why is someone else proposing my idea?

Description 1: My idea, your idea?

As business unit manager you are taking part in a management team meeting, in which you are the only woman. Passionate about your proposal to improve the cooperation between various departments, you put it forward during the round robin. There is hardly any response and your proposal is not discussed properly. To your surprise, at the next meeting, one of your colleagues repeats your proposal in different words and receives much acclaim. No one seems to remember the content of your proposal in the previous meeting. Your attempt to address the misappropriation of the idea and take back the initiative is blatantly ignored. You wonder how this happened.

Description 2: Power talk

During a management team meeting the strategic plan for a hostile takeover of a competitor is discussed at length. Due to bad investments the competitor is in financial difficulties and may well face dissolution or takeover. The atmosphere soon turns into 'us against them' and one of the directors, who holds a personal grudge against one of the directors of the company in trouble, states threateningly: 'We can force them to accept our offer since they have no alternative.' The meeting gradually takes the form of a personal vendetta instead of a rational exchange of business arguments. Rhetoric and power talk are rampant.

The only woman in the team has difficulty with the turn of events and tries to intervene and take the discussion back to its core: 'Why do you focus on the outside world instead of what's good for our clients? Shouldn't the key question be how our clients would benefit from this takeover instead of how we can make the life of our competitor miserable?'

Her male colleagues feel reprimanded, some get irritated, and others simply ignore her intervention and move on to the next point on the agenda. How can you get your message across in an atmosphere of power talk?

Description 3: Slapstick tactics

In a consultancy firm senior partners have acquired the habit of expressing their disappointment with certain events, such as missing out on an important client assignment, loudly and clearly. On this occasion, one of the senior partners is very angry because you made a mistake. He picks up a book and throws it across the room to you, yelling and shouting. Since this way of expressing disappointment is alien to you, you feel extremely uncomfortable and wonder how to react to this behavior.

Analysis

The three case studies provide examples of gender differences in language, but also of differences in the use of language as a tool in political games.

Men and women may use the same words while meaning different things. For instance, men often equate 'career success' with a good position, wealth, reputation, and title, so primarily external factors. For many women, 'career success' equates with an interesting job, work–life balance, pleasant colleagues, and opportunities for personal development, so more internal factors.

Missing broad-based support

In the first case study, the lack of preparation for the launch of your proposal is a key element for failure. In highly politicized organizations, who puts forward an idea may be more important than the content of the idea itself. Therefore, it is crucial to organize broad support for your proposal well in advance of the meeting.

Timing and seating

Finding the right time to pose an idea is an essential skill. An important proposal should not be put forward in the round robin, when the attention is gone and participants are collecting their papers to run out the door. Waiting to present a serious proposal until the last moment is bad timing and signals insufficient preparation.

Related to timing is the aspect of strategic seating. For an important proposal to receive the required attention you should make sure your position at the table is strategically located, for instance next to or opposite to the chairperson or one of the informal leaders of the team. This will give you the opportunity to stay in the lead when your proposal is discussed.

Creating a common enemy

Meeting cultures differ for each organization and each department. A commonly heard complaint from women is that meetings take too long, and that participants repeat themselves frequently and seem to be focused on hearing their own voice instead of having a dialogue with the others. In these corporate cultures the function of a meeting is rarely to organize operational tasks quickly, but more to create alliances and stimulate group feeling. In highly competitive cultures meetings take the form of an arena in which people are put in their places and the balance of power is tested continuously. Since different cultures require different behaviors, it is important to analyze a meeting culture before putting forward proposals of importance.

One of the ways of creating team spirit is to rally around a common enemy. The rhetoric in the second case study should be interpreted as way to create bonds between the group members and to investigate if 'everyone is on board'. Rhetoric and power talk are crucial elements in the decision-making rituals because they establish team support for the leader.

In the second case study, the female manager reacts to the situation as if the rhetoric should be taken literally. Her interpretation of the words is not in line with how they were intended by the speaker. In her view the interests of the company's clients are not taken seriously and the team's actions are driven by the wrong motives for the takeover. Throwing books across the room and uttering strong words, in the third case study, is a comparable way in which power talk and aggressive actions are used to mask frustration and disappointment.

The way in which men and women in the workplace express emotions like disappointment and anger can be very different. During a coaching session in my practice a CEO shared the feeling of powerlessness he had felt in a recent situation. One of his female team members started to cry when she had to report disappointing business results in the board meeting. He felt uncomfortable and did not know what the best response would have been. On the coach asking what his way of dealing with such a situation would have been, he confessed to regularly throwing objects around and using powerful language. It seems that many women internalize a disappointment, which may cause them to unintentionally start crying, whereas men seem to express themselves by strong language or vigorous action. Although the expressions are different, the underlying emotions are the same. It pays off to understand the differences in communication between genders and in cultures because it will enable you to be more effective in your communication.

Strategies

Create broad support

In politicized organizations you need to create support before putting your proposal forward in an official meeting. The first step is to discuss your proposal with a number of colleagues and listen carefully to suggestions and possible objections. It might be a good strategy to include a number of these suggestions in your proposal, together with the names of the reviewers.

Make sure your proposal is tabled at the right time during the meeting. Setting the agenda is the prerogative of the chairperson, the secretary, or informal leaders, so you need to gather their support in advance. Your internal network can help you get your proposal on the right place on the agenda, too.

If the proposal contains alterations to the company's structure or will have a significant impact on employees, it is advisable to seek the support of those who will back certain parts of the proposal based on their expertise. Investigate the possibility of working in cooperation with some of the team members in order to jointly put forward some of the aspects of the proposal. By discussing the proposal with the key informal leaders in the organization you will create support not only at the meeting, but also more broadly across the organization. This will prove useful when your proposal will have impact on others outside of your own span of control.

A good preparation requires an assessment of the implicit hierarchy at the meeting: who speaks first and who is likely to support whom. It is useful to consider if some members have the habit of supporting or undermining each other regardless of the content of any proposal.

A useful tactic is to set up an exchange between your support for someone else's proposal against his or hers for yours. However, you should avoid finding yourself in a situation in which you have to second a motion that you would normally fiercely oppose.

Use strategic language

The use of language is unique in organizations and is part of corporate culture. From coaching sessions and workshops it appears that many women unconsciously choose nice and friendly words without always realizing what the impact might be. The knowledge and ability to adapt the use of words to your environment is an essential part of the toolkit of skills for leadership positions. This does not mean that you have to adopt power or bossy language, but that you become aware of situations when you need to adapt your speech in order to realize your goals.

Table 7.1 contains simple examples of the effective use of language in politicized organizations, male-dominated cultures, and those with a lack of women in senior positions. The texts have been oversimplified and exaggerated to make contrasts clear.

In the *first column* you will find the literal text, such as in the first example: 'If you have time, could you perhaps do this for me?'

The *second column* describes the intention of the speaker. In this example it is the intention of the manager to 'not be bossy or unkind' when she asks her employee to do something for her.

The *third column* demonstrates that the audience might interpret the text differently from the speaker's intended meaning. It is very possible that in the example people will think 'she is not very assertive' and tie this qualification to a negative judgment of her leadership qualities as manager.

In the *fourth column* you will find suggestions for alternative texts that might be more effective in this culture. The tone of voice should be adapted too from friendly high-pitched to serious and professional. Adapting the original text to stronger language which is common in this culture creates more respect. The alternative text in this example – 'Can you do this now?' – seems to differ not so much but will definitely influence the perception of your qualities as manager in this environment.

TABLE 7.1 Strategic use of language			
Text	**Intention**	**Interpretation**	**Alternative text**
'If you have time, could you perhaps do this for me?'	*Giving instructions is bossy or unkind*	Leader lacks assertiveness, is too nice	**'Can you do this now?'**
'In 2010 we realized significant growth in revenue'	*Saying 'I' is boastful*	Leader lacks ownership of her role as leader	**'I realized 25 percent growth in revenue in 2010' or 'With my team I am responsible for achieving 25 percent growth in revenue in 2010'**
'I am so sorry for being late!'	*Leader is concerned about what others think*	Leader lacks authority because she apologizes	**'Thank you for waiting' or 'Let's start right away'**
'I think we should implement this idea'	*Being self-confident is bossy*	Leader is insecure, lacks self-confidence and is incompetent	**'I am going to implement this' or 'This will be implemented right away'**

Building on the schedule, additional main points for effective communication in assimilation and accommodation cultures are:

- Restrict the number of verbs in your sentences and concentrate on describing concrete outcomes and results.
- Always use numbers to qualify your statements (increase, turnover, personnel, budget, and so on).

- Avoid speaking on behalf of 'us' and do not use 'we' too often. Regularly use 'I' to emphasize your responsibilities.
- Use past tense for achievements, and present and future tenses for your plans.
- Avoid using words that undermine your statement, for example, 'perhaps', 'maybe', 'right'.
- Use active sentences instead of passive ones, so you demonstrate being in control.
- Avoid inserting doubts in your statements through words such as 'I think', 'I don't know', 'I am not certain of . . .' or conjugations such as 'should', 'could', 'would'.

Develop effective meeting behavior

Proper preparation for meetings ensures that your ideas will be taken seriously. The following tactics can be useful:

- Choose a strategic position in relation to the chairperson at the table, such as opposite or next to him or her.
- Take a relaxed but alert posture without leaning over or sitting on the tip of your chair.
- Hold your head straight (tilting gives the impression of begging) and keep your body still (instead of wiggling and fumbling).
- Be conscious of the fact that smiling too much may undermine your credibility. Stop smiling when you address an important topic, and show in your posture that you take yourself seriously.
- Don't clean up other people's mess. If someone spills coffee at the other end of the table, refrain from cleaning it up.
- 'Break the rules' from time to time, for instance by taking the seat at the head of the table.

Why do they ask me to deliver bad news?

Description

A female consultant is working in a project team. One of the senior team members is not pulling his weight and because he is more senior she gradually picks up more and more of his tasks. The team leader notices this development and praises her for her flexibility and dedication to the project. The situation deteriorates until finally the team leader decides to remove the unwilling team member from his team. He invites the female consultant to give her opinion on how to deliver the bad news. She feels recognized for her contribution and professionalism and is proud that the team leader values her opinion. So she eagerly volunteers to explain how she would approach this sensitive situation. Before she knows it, the team leader proposes that she will deliver the bad news. He is convinced she can do a good job because her people-management skills are very impressive and the way she communicates naturally about sensitive issues has been an asset to the project.

Delighted by his praise she accepts the task to deliver the bad news.

Analysis

Frequently, women share the experience that their male colleagues ask them to break the bad news in work situations. Reasons cited are that women, apparently, are better equipped to deal with people's emotions in difficult circumstances and that their more human approach will benefit the situation. Since bad news conversations are an inherent part of the toolkit of management skills, it is not always clear if the intentions in situations such as the one above are honest and in the interest of the company. Many women report that afterward they felt that they had been taken for a ride.

A key question in such situations is to ask: 'Will I gain or lose respect by accepting these unpopular tasks?' It may well be that your intentions are to help the company, whereas the person who asks this favor only wants to get rid of a difficult job. The latter will clearly not lead to respect. It is important to investigate how people in the company view this.

Strategies

Resist flattery

First, you need to analyze your sensitivity to flattery. The issue at stake, to deliver a difficult message on behalf of someone else, is a professional service asked by a colleague. In professional relationships there is no room for passing the buck to someone else. Be aware of flattery being used to have you accept an assignment you should not.

Turn weakness into strength

Your expertise to deliver difficult messages can be an important skill in the advancement of your career. By developing this competency it becomes an asset instead of a weakness, which can be useful in achieving your strategic goals.

When you are approached to be the bearer of bad news again, analyze what favor you can ask for from the other party. It might be an introduction to someone of importance to your career or to put in a good word with your manager. Another way of promoting yourself as professional in this situation is to agree that it will be made public how crucial your intervention has been. Lastly, make sure that your expertise receives sufficient positive attention by explicitly discussing it during evaluation sessions with your manager.

Break the rules

The case can also be symptomatic of a lack of respect for you as a professional. If you always get the difficult assignments no one volunteers for, you may suffer from a case of extreme 'pleasing' behavior. You need to take back control through breaking the rules. Be unpredictable and say 'no' to a difficult assignment. Have faith in your qualities as a professional and don't be bothered by the fact that not everyone will like you anymore. In strong assimilation cultures, this behavior signals strength and confidence, and commands respect. Make sure that you only solve someone else's problem when it is worth it so you gain respect.

For instance, if you are not allowed to hire new employees because of cost-cutting programs and you notice that others still do, break the rule too. Many women want to play by the rules and admirably continue to act in the interest of the company as a whole. However, their reluctance to say 'no' and unwillingness to break the rules from time to time may well lead to an overload of work in contrast with their colleagues.

Personal attacks

Personal attacks are painful and discouraging. Women report that as they progress through the ranks and become more successful it appears that personal attacks increase. How can you effectively deal with this?

Why do I suffer personal attacks?

Description

After an extensive executive search process, a female IT professional is appointed to the executive board of an international listed company as chief information officer. Although 40 percent of the employees and most of the customers are women, she is the first and only woman on the board. It has been the company's policy to actively search for a woman for this position to make a statement to employees and its client base. After a while the female board member is showing excellent performance and her activities clearly add value to the company. She is considered to be at least partially responsible for the improvements in the company's reputation and subsequently the share price. In the board meetings she receives open recognition for her contribution. However, gradually she discovers that her subordinates are experiencing difficulties in getting things organized. Small conflicts appear and seem to multiply. In addition, senior executives outside her direct hierarchical line are starting to oppose her plans, although in the board her colleagues still support her. The initial criticism on the content of her proposals becomes more personal and focused on her private life and leadership style. The situation escalates further and in the end she decides to leave the company. Her successor appears to have been waiting at the sideline already.

What could she have done differently?

Analysis

Being the outsider

The most important competencies for top positions are the ability to build and exercise power (*Power*) and organize (self-)promotion (*Promotion*). Being recruited from the outside for a top position is often far more challenging than progressing through the ranks. It takes a considerable amount of time and effort to develop the essential power networks. Building relationships within and outside of the company is crucial for the success of the position.

In this case study, the female board member clearly struggles with becoming part of the formal and informal networks and appears to remain an outsider during her tenure. It also may well be that the influential informal networks had pushed forward an internal candidate that had been identified before the executive search was started.

Role model

The fact that she was the first and only woman on the executive board and the public PR campaign around it could impact in several ways. As the only woman, she may feel extra pressure to perform. As a role model, perhaps even against her will, she is the representative of all female employees in the company. Because of the uniqueness of her position, she attracts more attention than her colleagues. If she fails, it may damage the reputation of the company, creating the image of a female-unfriendly company. Furthermore, if she fails the hidden criticism that she was appointed to the board 'only because she was a woman' will become more public. All of these factors may make it more difficult for all other women in the company to advance their careers.

Personal attacks

Personal attacks occur when the support system in the form of informal networks that channel criticism fails. In this case study she openly receives the support of the board but not outside, which hinders her staff from performing to the best of their abilities. It is important to investigate the source of the covert opposition and discover who is or are behind the flow of criticism and why. Personal attacks may also be a sign that you are considered to be difficult to approach or do not welcome advice or support.

Strategies

Prepare a professional plan for the first 100 days

In the first three months in a new position you lay the foundation for the implementation of the plans you have been hired for. The first priority is the acquisition of relevant knowledge about the company, its markets, products and services, the internal organization, and employees. In addition, it is essential to develop connections with all important stakeholders, such as shareholders, the supervisory board, authorities, advisors, and financiers, but also with external contacts, such as accountants, general counsel, works council, and any interest groups. One of the key activities in the first 100 days is to assess the quality of your personnel and their fit with your vision and implementation plans. Inevitably, some staff will become redundant and new talent will need to be recruited.

Develop your power and promotion competencies

Personal attacks are a sign of having insufficient support in informal networks of importance. Therefore, your second priority is becoming integrated into these networks as soon as possible. It is essential to quickly establish a group of confidants who are able to shed a different light on personal criticisms based on their own personal experiences with you. This mechanism will protect you from malicious attacks and better equip you to shape your reputation and image in the company.

The starting point for the development of a strategic network at top level are your direct colleagues and board members; since theoretically all will benefit from your appointment becoming a success they will be inclined to help you establish some crucial contacts. For charting the relevant networks and connections you can consult internal sources and external ones, for example Google and LinkedIn. (Chapter 10 contains additional tools to develop strategic networking skills.) After gaining understanding of the way connections are linked and which networks provide crucial information, your peers and board members may provide you with introductions to key people.

Be proactive in bringing forward which networks you belong to yourself and which of your connections might be of relevance to the company. Organizing a meeting in which all board members chart their networks and jointly discuss which specific connections might be of strategic importance to the company is a very useful exercise. Opening up your own networks to your colleagues creates goodwill and accelerates the process of becoming integrated in the most essential networks.

Play the part

In the case study it becomes clear that being the first and only female board member has reputational and PR value for the company. Although some top women are reluctant to play this card, it can be very useful for establishing your own reputation and building connections with parties outside of the company. Accepting speaking engagements, interviews, and attending public events are part of the function of a 'role model'. If you do this well and the company's reputation benefits from it, your promotional power may cause criticisms to disappear.

Reorganizations

Statistics indicate that in most countries more men than women are losing their job in the current economic crisis.[3] This is caused by the fact that the crisis is hitting the sectors in which men tend to be employed (e.g. construction and manufacturing) the hardest. However, part-time workers are among those most at risk. Since part-time work is primarily taken up by women, many are losing their jobs now too.

In this case study a number of issues will be addressed. Which competencies do we need to survive a crisis situation in an organization? How to turn crisis situations into opportunities?

Why do I lose my job in the reorganization?

Description

After a number of loss-making years, management announces the implementation of a radical reorganization plan which will lead to the loss of 10 percent of all jobs. The company's intranet does not contain any detailed information on the plans and simply refers employees to their manager for questions.

Unsuspectingly, a female account manager, who recently cut down her working days to four for a limited period of time, attends the 'town hall meeting' at which management will provide details of the plans. Half an hour before the start of the meeting one of her colleagues mentions that her manager has put her name forward for the list of redundancies. Surprised by the news she asks her colleague about the criteria and hears that apparently she is not the only part-time employee on the list. Since her track record is excellent and her tenure is long, she wonders how she can prevent losing her job.

Analysis

Impact of the crisis

From many discussions with HR directors a pattern emerges showing that in many large companies women are the first ones to leave when a crisis hits or structural reorganizations are implemented. The following factors come into play:

- *Content above politics*
  Women are often more focused on the content of the job and the possibilities to grow and develop their skills. The prospect of having to devote substantial amounts of time to politics and lobbying in the reorganization process does not appeal to them. HR directors report that women are twice as likely to accept severance pay packages as their male counterparts. This may be influenced by the fact that men are often still the breadwinner of the household and, therefore, more inclined to fight for their position than women.

- *Structural causes*
  The under-representation of women in decision-making positions leads to their voices not being heard at the table where decisions about the reorganization take place. Very few companies put their restructuring plans to the test regarding the (intended and unintended) effect on their female employees.

- *The part-time effect*
  In the decision-making processes about redundancy packages, part-time employees are often considered to be more expensive and less efficient than full-time employees. Since women dominate in part-time work, consequently, they will be disproportionately over-represented on the redundancies list.

- *Lack of strategic information*
  Women are often not part of the informal networks in which the decisions are prepared, so their influence is limited. In addition, their absence puts them in a disadvantageous position because the information about the likelihood where the reorganization will hit hardest is not shared with them. Without this crucial information they are less able to operate strategically by, for example, putting in a request for a transfer to another part of the company that will be less affected or influencing the decision-making process about the redundancies.

One of the advantages of being part of the informal networks is that members share knowledge about important events such as a restructuring. Because of the confidentiality of the information it is often shared very subtly through hints. The expression 'no one is indispensable' might be such a way of informing a colleague who is on the redundancies list but does not know this yet.

- *Social pressure*
  Some women leave the company during reorganization due to social pressures. It is not uncommon for women to be confronted with the message that their job could be done by a man who has to provide for his family. In some cultures it is acceptable to openly address this factor and even include it in the official decision-making process. These social pressures force women, especially when they have an employed partner, to accept severance pay quicker than they would normally.

Strategies

Discover your crisis competency

Review which unique competencies you have, their value for your current position, and their value for the organization you work for. Find answers to the question 'What makes you the best person for this job?' Put aside any feelings of modesty and concentrate on your uniqueness and excellence in performance.

This process is similar to the one companies embark upon regularly to establish and develop their competitive advantage and their uniqueness. An interesting example is Sony, the Japanese company that until 2003 concentrated on producing sound equipment, building on its invention of the transistor radio. Increasing competition and globalization of markets put significant pressure on the company's results. A fundamental review of its core competencies led to the conclusion that its core competency was no longer the production of sound equipment, but the ability to miniaturize high-quality technical components.

Like companies analyzing their *core competencies* you may embark on a similar process by analyzing your unique skills. What makes you stand out among others? Examples of unique leadership competencies are multiple: the ability to handle complexity (of decision-making, techniques, or organizations); the capability to connect with people and organizations; or the power to inspire and motivate people. These competencies are unique and can be applied in many functions and organizations. Being able to answer the question why you are still the best person for the job after the reorganization makes you more prepared and confident to lobby. In addition, it also opens your mind for new possibilities in or outside the company.

Develop staying power

Some people in organizations seem untouchable. They are not affected by reorganization and always survive in the same or even a better job, as if they were covered in a non-stick coating. Their ability to survive in crisis situations and often benefit from them is called 'staying power'. Staying power is a variation of the power networks, as described in 7.2 above. Like an invisible force it protects you against the negative impact of reorganizations but also when a personal attack is launched during a meeting. You may not even know in person the individuals who protect your interests and lobby on your behalf.

Staying power carries an element of 'promise' and an iron-clad trust of others in your capacities and skills. The impact is that your perceived value is higher than your actual value since the connections give you a certain amount of power. Staying power refers to authority and the notion that 'you can't do this to him or her'. It builds on your external and internal networks, and its weight depends on the status and strength of your contacts. The ability to promote yourself has an impact on your staying power, too. An important element of developing staying power is reciprocity. Since every connection puts their own interests first, you can only develop staying power if you add value to the other's interests. It is an unwritten rule that if you help someone, he or she will help you next time.

Staying power can have negative effects, too. In organizations in which large groups of people with staying power block new ideas and new people, organizational development is seriously hindered. Symptomatic is the appointment of people who are not the most qualified candidates to certain senior positions and the bypassing of qualified employees who are not part of the informal networks. A culture of compromising on the quality of people in the interest of protecting the interests of a small group will harm the business in the long run.

Most favored positions

In every organization people know which functions are the best and most sought-after. These positions often combine a few attractive elements, such as a relatively large degree of freedom, budget or expense account, external representation (invitations to interesting conferences, meetings, and events), an impressive title and, more importantly, access to the inner circle, the informal network of the organization. Although these positions may not always technically qualify as 'top level' jobs, in the formal hierarchy they are considered influential and are only given to employees who are expected to reach top positions later in their career. Examples of these functions are key positions in reorganization or acquisition teams, with a high degree of decision-making power, but also expatriate contracts for upcoming countries or in popular business lines, with highly attractive terms of employment.

Why do I miss out on the most favored positions?

Description

A female senior manager who has been with a financial services company for over ten years has expressed her ambition to continue to grow professionally and ultimately be appointed to the board. Since line-management and expatriate experience are requirements for board positions, she develops a strategic plan to land an expatriate assignment. She is convinced that the experience of managing people in a different culture and environment will significantly enhance her leadership capabilities. Expatriate contracts are rare, very sought-after, and therefore very difficult to secure. To increase her chances of success she puts in a request for a transfer to a region that is less popular because of the challenges in normal life (e.g. insecurity, unfavorable climate, and rampant corrupt business practices). She started her career with another company, working for five years in this region, so she is well aware of the culture and pitfalls in doing business over there. She is convinced that her five years of regional experience and her ten years in line management with the current company make her the best-qualified candidate for the posting. As the management development department coordinates the selection of candidates for overseas assignments, she sets up an appointment. To her surprise the interview is canceled a few days before the date, and the same happens to her second appointment. A few weeks later the company announces the transfer to her desired job of one of her colleagues, who she knows never even visited the region. She has difficulty believing that he is a better candidate and wonders what she could have done differently to secure this position.

Analysis

An important characteristic of these sought-after functions is that they are generally not widely or publicly advertised. The procedure for candidate selection often lacks transparency and is therefore difficult to influence. Especially for positions that are considered training grounds for future top management, the informal networks play a crucial or decisive part in the procedures.

Strategies

Address the issue of transparency

The first strategy at policy level is to demand more transparency around these types of vacancies. Improving the transparency of the available vacancies, the application criteria, and the selection procedure has a proven positive effect on the advancement of women to higher positions in general.

Informal networking

One of the reasons for the senior manager in this case study missing out on the desired position is the apparent absence of informal networking, demonstrated by her reliance on the formal selection procedure through the management development department. The impact of the informal network is that it generates broad support for your candidacy. In addition, it enables you to gather extra information about the vacancy and your competitors. Lastly, the informal network provides the opportunity to be pre-informed about next vacancies for interesting positions and the best way to approach the selection procedure. Informal networking is therefore crucial in preparing your strategy to successfully apply for the most sought-after positions.

Strategy of the swallows

An interesting strategy is 'schwalben' or the strategy of the swallows. 'Schwalben' is a German verb describing the behavior of a flock of swallows suddenly dropping down to a lower level in the atmosphere to continue their journey. In soccer, the term 'schwalbe' is used for a player's provocation of an offence by an opponent on the field. It is a very subtle attempt to mislead the referee by making him think the other party committed the offence, resulting in a penalty benefiting the player who made the schwalbe. The fact that an innocent party gets penalized is of no interest to the person using this strategy. The resemblance with a straightforward dirty trick is obvious owing to the fact that both actions are aimed at gaining a personal advantage over another person. However, what sets them apart is the gracious movement and theatre play accompanying the schwalbe. A schwalbe is as gracious as the swallows in the sky. Outsiders watching a schwalbe revel in its beauty and creativity. It is not only about gaining an advantage in the game, but also how. As a consequence, a schwalbe is easily forgiven and even fiercely defended against claims of it just being a dirty trick. Developing the competency to use schwalbes is therefore a crucial part of your career toolkit.

The following example demonstrates the power of this technique. A successful schwalbe starts with the identification of the interesting position you would like to land. Through your informal networks you find out that currently the position is being fulfilled by someone who is not functioning well due to personal circumstances. Use the personal information you have gained subtly by feeding it to people who are sensitive to it. Always make sure that confidential information can never be traced back to you because you will then soon be found out and rightly accused of pulling a dirty trick. In the case of an underperforming employee, a good strategy is to subtly express your concerns about results lagging behind or potential damage to the company's interests if the underperformance continues for much longer. Part of the schwalbe strategy is to get personally involved in the situation under the pretence of helping out. A talented user of this strategy is a master in simulating genuine sympathy.

The second part of the schwalbe strategy is to promote your suitability for the position to decision-makers responsible for selecting the successor for this interesting job. Since you may not have direct access to them or do not want to be in the spotlight for the schwalbe you are setting up, you need to rely on your informal network to promote your qualities and achievements. For positions of strategic importance the element of trust often plays an important role in the selection of a successor. It is imperative to spend considerable amounts of time in the informal circuits of the decision-makers in order for them to get acquainted with you and build up trust in the relationship. If trust is the decisive factor you cannot rely on your excellent track record and top-quality education to land this interesting job.

The third part of the schwalbe is to continue to connect and develop close ties with the person you would like to succeed and make sure your positive relationship is noticed in the informal circuit. Be aware that your true intentions remain private and prevent exaggeration in the process. If executed well, either the person whose position you are after or people around this person will ask you if you can help out more regularly. This is the best opportunity to learn the ropes and prepare for the day of your official nomination. You have succeeded in your schwalbe strategy if no one is surprised at the formal announcement of your taking over the sought-after position.

Some will frown over the example of a successful schwalbe strategy. The admiration for its perfect execution clashes with the feeling that it may not be fair to go to such lengths for a much-desired position. How can you be an authentic leader and use strategies like schwalbes at the same time? On the other hand, is it authentic and realistic to not adapt to a certain culture, decline the use of accepted strategies, and rely on ineffective behaviors and . . . still expect to obtain the most sought-after positions?

CHAPTER 8

Career

8.1 Taking the Silk Road to the Top

Metaphors are powerful tools of communication. They connect expressive images with daily concepts or events. For far too long metaphors about women and leadership have been negative and victimizing. Coined in 1986 in the *Wall Street Journal* as a metaphor for the invisible barriers to career advancement women encounter, the 'glass ceiling' is still popular today. Based on the notion that gender stereotypes create a network of constraints and interpersonal reactions, it has inspired a host of glass barriers, from the glass cliff[1] to glass borders and glass escalators,[2] as explanations for the absence of women in top positions.[3] Another catchphrase is that a host of obstacles prevent women from reaching the C-suite while they struggle through 'the labyrinth of leadership'.[4]

However, society has changed dramatically in a generation and women have entered the workplace in vast numbers. In the United States more women than men are currently employed. Although the numbers of women in top positions are still lagging behind, women are taking charge in shaping their own routes to the top now. Therefore, it is time to change the negative metaphors and discover a new one. The metaphor of the Silk Road to the Top conveys a *positive and inspiring message*.

From marching route to Silk Road

The Silk Road consisted of an extensive network of trade routes in the Middle Ages, connecting 'the East' (Asia) and 'the West' (Europe). This ancient route had a significant impact on our culture and our economies, and helped lay the foundations for modern civilization. Two worlds were connected and trade flourished. From the East valuable goods such as silk, jewels, and spices were transported to the West. The Silk Road had a profound influence on the cultures of both worlds, which resulted in an increase in prosperity worldwide and the development of great civilizations.

From logical and linear ... to fluid and flexible careers

The metaphor of the Silk Road to the Top in the business world refers to the opposite of the traditional marching route: the hierarchical, linear, and logical path to the top of an organization. Women often follow different roads to the top than the traditional ones. More women than men have to deal with shorter or longer career breaks, periods of part-time work because of caring responsibilities, and volunteer work.

Organizations are quickly evolving from ancient, hierarchical, pyramidal structures, in which successful careers are characterized by loyalty and lifetime employment, to flat and flexible structures, in which project work and career switches have become the norm and no longer the exception to the rule. The Silk Road to the Top is therefore becoming more accessible to all – women and men alike.

Travel requirements

For travellers the Silk Route was adventurous because they entered unknown territory and met people with different habits who spoke a foreign language. The dangers and hardship experienced during the trip were offset against the promise and realization of considerable rewards. To succeed on the Silk Road you needed fierce resilience and solid planning, alongside a top-quality team and excellent materials and resources. These requirements still hold true for women's Silk Road to the Top in organizations.

Challenges and choices

International research shows that women are experiencing their route to the top differently than men.[5] Women report encountering greater challenges than their male counterparts, such as having to adapt to the tone at the top, the corporate culture, and often the exclusion from informal networks. They also recognize that it is more important for them to have an excellent track record and to build up a network of internal and external relationships that will help them along in their career.

The top women currently employed in the Fortune 100 companies have reached their position in different ways than their male colleagues. They are younger, less frequently 'lifetime employees', have spent less time in every job, and have climbed the ranks faster than their average male counterpart.[6]

Increasing connectivity

The over-representation of women in supporting roles as opposed to leading and managing roles makes it less likely for many of them to reach the top of organizations.

Research into the background of supervisory board members is revealing a pattern which indicates that the Silk Road, as the metaphor connecting two worlds of male and female leadership, is intensifying. Corporations are increasingly appointing female supervisory or non-executive board members from other disciplines and sectors than the business world. Many current female board members have a background in government, politics, academia, non-governmental organizations, and public organizations. Confronted with a shortage of women with experience in top management positions in companies, and the need to heed the call from press, public, and governments to appoint more women on boards, nowadays the net is being cast in a wide variety of sectors and even abroad. The Silk Road to the Top is therefore becoming more and more popular.

Generating prosperity

The Silk Road generating prosperity for all as a result of the connection between two worlds also applies to the corporate world. Companies with a substantial share of women in top management (at least 30 percent) outperform those with few or no women. Despite the fact that causality has not been proven, numerous studies in various countries report similar results and are therefore being taken seriously.[7] In many studies there is a clear indication that a high percentage of women in top management is leading to more financial gain for all stakeholders. What's more, the quality of corporate governance and decision-making is reported to improve significantly.[8] So the connection between women and men in leadership leads to more prosperity, just like the ancient Silk Road did.

Finesse and flexibility

An important element of the metaphor of the Silk Road to the Top can be found in the new leadership styles. Silk has a number of characteristics that are frequently attributed to women, such as softness combined with strength, colorfulness (in the sense of being different from prevailing patterns), and flexibility as a fabric. These features could be translated into leadership competencies such as the ability to adapt, flexibility, and responsiveness. Silk embodies finesse and an eye for detail. When applied to leadership styles, there is a sharp contrast with the ancient, typically masculine, leadership style of the generals and their traditional marching orders for their followers. The current generation of female leaders is no longer inclined to copy the symbols of male power in their behavior and dress. The pinstriped suit has made way for a new sophisticated style. Color and flexibility are being appreciated now, too. Even in the most conservative industry sectors a transformation is taking place, whereby women follow their own career paths and on their own terms.

Inclusive leadership as a connection

The vision to connect two worlds – the East and the West, masculine and feminine leadership qualities, and men and women in teams – is a core competence of inclusive leaders. The pillar of inclusive leadership, explained in Chapter 6, is the acknowledgment of differences (in culture, background, experience, gender, style, religion, and so on). It is defined by actively engaging in these differences in order to reach the highest quality of decision-making. All differences are embraced and any deviations from standard patterns are used as a tool to generate a variety of viewpoints and input for the dialogue. The style builds on the premise that the complementary nature of different traits, backgrounds, and views will lead to the highest quality of decision-making. Appointing people whom we are comfortable working with and with whom we feel 'in sync' often enables a relatively quick and uncomplicated decision-making process. However, to ensure the continuity of an organization it is necessary to consciously create the conditions for high-quality decision-making, not only in the short term, but especially in the long term. Through dialogue and free exchange of arguments, the best decision in a specific situation will develop naturally.

Success on the Silk Road in the Middle Ages was dependent on three key elements. These elements are still relevant for today's journey in the business world.

1. *Perfection in planning*

   A good planning process starts with formulating the milestones in your career: Where do you want to be in five years' time? How do you want to achieve your goals, in a straight line or with stops and detours along the way? Your planning also depends on making a solid analysis of the knowledge and support you will need. A realistic planning process takes into account unforeseen circumstances and includes sufficient flexibility to deal with them or to adjust your goals if necessary. Defining short-term targets along the way ensures that the road to the top remains manageable and clear.

2. *Top team*

For many business women a good planning process does not only include organizing the knowledge needed (through education and training) and building up relevant experience. The ability to recruit and lead talented individuals and create coalitions with team members and outsiders is as crucial. The key component of your top team may well be your support system at home. Since no one reaches the top on her own, building a top team around you is of crucial importance.

3. *Toolkit of skills*

A top-quality toolkit ensures that you stay connected to yourself on the way to the top and that you use your competencies as effectively and efficiently as possible, without wasting energy and intelligence. Communication and negotiation skills should be among the most developed tools. The toolkit of skills includes navigation skills, for instance the ability to steer away from dangerous situations in which you are vulnerable and the ability to observe what is happening around you. A 20/20 vision in combination with the courage for self-reflection and ability to put things into perspective should be part of the toolkit. Every stop in a different country is a challenge in terms of culture, habits, and language. The mindset and courage to be open-minded toward differences without judging them or wanting to change them is an indispensable trait for success.

8.2 FAQs

Take the image of an ice skater participating in the famous Dutch Eleven Cities skating tour who is forced to leave the ice because of blowholes and who struggles to continue the journey on land. Ice skates are not for walking; on land they are cumbersome, slow, and could potentially lead to injuries or accidents. Walking on skates on land involves working hard, against the odds, with inadequate means. It takes far more strength and different muscles than the skater trained for. Sheer determination and willpower are prerequisites to reach the next station on the route.

You may recognize this image as a metaphor and feel that you sometimes seem to have to work harder than men who seem to encounter fewer blowholes and continue to glide to the top. How do you prevent having to walk on land to the top?

The frequently asked questions on the topic of career advancement that will be analyzed in this chapter are:

- Why do they always ask me for supporting instead of leading roles?
- Why did I miss this promotion?
- Why do I not get the credit I deserve?
- Why do they often approach me for difficult tasks?
- How do I successfully land a board position?

The first FAQ is undoubtedly the most popular one and is often asked the first time women realize that they have put too much faith in the myth of meritocracy. The last FAQ is a generic topic which will be dealt with in a general context.

Successful career paths

Various career paths lead to the top. Analyzing the career paths of the top managers in an organization will provide insights into which are the most successful career choices. In most companies the top positions are reserved for people with ample experience in *line management* (managing people) and with so-called *profit and loss responsibility*. The ability to take crucial decisions which affect bottom-line results is a prerequisite for senior functions.

A second requirement in many organizations is that candidates have ample experience of working and living abroad. This so-called *expatriate experience* is considered to be a reliable test of one's independence and capacity to survive in difficult circumstances. The experience teaches leaders to be effective in an environment characterized by other values, habits, and communication styles. The ability to adapt to changes in the environment without feeling threatened is a key learning experience of expatriate managers. Since relatively few women have both line-management and expatriate experience, this is often cited as one of the most important reasons for the under-representation of women in top management.

A career in supporting roles seldom guarantees the achievement of a top position in the corporate world. There are very few examples of CEOs who have come through the ranks of human resources, like former CEO of DSM, Peter Elverding. Very few boards have appointed a chief HR officer at board level.

In addition, many women experience that the way back to line management is blocked if they deviate from the road to the top by accepting a position in supporting roles. Since most top positions in the supporting roles are taken by men, it is also difficult for women to reach the top in the hierarchy of supporting units.

Another issue to investigate before choosing a career path is the existence of other *implicit hierarchies*. In large international corporations there might be an implicit or formal hierarchy between local and head-office responsibilities, and in specialist functions such as legal services or accounting. A career move from a local specialist role to a role in head office or a position of central responsibility is often considered to be a promotion and on the path to the top. The role of chief financial officer (CFO) in a small local business unit might be seen as less challenging than the equivalent role in a large business unit, but it may well be a better career move if the smaller unit is in one of the strategic growth areas, as opposed to the larger unit being considered as takeover material.

Why do they always ask me for supporting rather than leading roles?

Description

A young female engineer was employed by an international oil company as leader of a project team responsible for managing one of the oil pipelines in a difficult area. Her role was comparable to a business unit management role, with responsibility for financial results of the project. Her career progressed well and in line with the internal criteria for talent development. While preparing for the next step in her career she was approached to move to the department of management development (human resources), with the specific task of developing a new company program for international management trainees. The selection committee considered her apparent lack of knowledge and experience in this field as unimportant. Her defence that the proposed role was not part of her own career planning and that she lacked ambition for it was noted. The main reason behind this proposed career move was that it would make her a more balanced manager because management development required different people skills than the ones she had relied on until now. Within the company this career move was not considered to be a logical step for people who had the ambition to grow into serious senior management roles.

She was completely surprised and shocked by the proposal. She wondered what she had done wrong and how she could correct her apparent mistakes.

Analysis

Her surprise over the proposal could be caused by a variety of reasons.

Unaware of your capabilities

Too often women will accept the reasons for the proposal and move to the new role thinking: 'If they say it will benefit me, they are probably right.' This way of thinking emerges when you do not have full understanding of your competencies and how others in the company perceive you. The learning opportunities the new role offers may well be important for your development as all-round leader, so the proposal deserves serious contemplation. However, the arguments by the selection committee should provide more information on this than given in this case study. The general statement that it will benefit your career is not a sufficient reason to accept such a radical proposal. You may expect a selection committee to fully explain its reasons for approaching you and how the career move will benefit your leadership development.

Safe choice

In some corporate cultures there is less opposition toward women in supporting roles than in leadership roles. In such cultures a choice to accept a role in management development is actually a safe choice. You may find it easier to operate in this role than in a business unit management role. In some companies the option of a 'safe choice' is also actively used in career management as a tool to accommodate managers (men and women) if they want to temporarily leave the career track due to personal circumstances.

(Perceived) lack of ambition

The situation described in the case study could be a symptom of a lack of career planning and strategic direction. Without a clear ambition to develop your skills, people may perceive you as lacking ambition. Formulating your leadership statement (Chapter 2) is the first step to improving your sense of direction.

Ineffective communication

The cause of the situation may lie in the lack of proper and timely communication about your ambition and career plans. If you have not informed key people of your aspirations, they will not be taken into account. This increases the chance that assumptions will dominate other people's discussions and decisions about your career. It is a well-known pattern among women to only start thinking of next steps and promotions after you have mastered all the details of the current job. Unfortunately, this may well be too late, as shown in the case study. Lastly, your ambitions may not have reached the decision-makers in the company because you are unknown in the informal networks.

Strategies

Provided your plan is to stay with the company, you have several options. The first five strategies provide ideas to capitalize on your current situation. The last strategy describes a scenario in which you fight the appointment, which may ultimately lead you to leave the company.

Take time

Refrain from being pushed into taking a decision immediately during the conversation with the selection committee. Indicate you need time to seriously contemplate the offer on the table. A much-used management technique is to put pressure on the candidate to decide on the spot. Often, an atmosphere of confidentiality and trust is created, which may seduce you to answer immediately. Resist the urge to give a first reaction or initial response, and refrain from giving clues as to your likely answer. Repeat your willingness to investigate the proposal on the table and give a clear time frame for your final answer. Always keep the option open for an additional meeting to discuss more details before you can agree or reject the proposal.

Investigate the origin

Investigate the procedures that are normally followed for the selection and recruitment of this type of function. Find out if there are always more candidates for this role or whether, due to the lack of spontaneous candidates, the committee actively searches for candidates and appoints one. Investigate who has put forward your name. Make an inventory of the committee members and their background and relationships in order to find out who actually knows you or knows someone you worked with closely. Collect as much feedback as possible from your colleagues, managers, and subordinates to understand what image you have in the company. This will probably provide clues as to why you have been approached for this specific role in the first place. Match this image with your own and address any gaps between them.

In some companies, supporting roles are less prestigious and do not attract the top talents. Investigate how your new department or role is perceived. Find out in which departments high potentials and top talents are appointed.

Contact the committee chair to gain more understanding of the content of the job and try to discover the potential strategic aspects of the role. Match the elements of the role with elements in your personal leadership development plan in order to continue your development in this new role. Formulate these elements and discuss them with the committee and your new manager.

Prepare your path for return

As your ambition to continue on the managerial route clearly has not been communicated properly to parties involved, start a communication campaign on concrete milestones and activities you would like to pursue in your next job.

If you want to continue on the managerial road, consider negotiating a time limit for your new job and a promise that you will return to your aspired path afterward. Make sure this agreement is documented properly.

Set specific goals in your new role which are related to your long-term career path. This indicates that you appreciate the opportunity for further leadership development the new role offers, but at the same time signals your resolve to not become a specialist in this field and your intention to return to managerial roles.

Develop transferable skills

Continue to speak the language of executives in your new role. Concentrate on activities which could be of long-term interest for your career. Avoid activities in the back office and those that have no relevance to managerial functions, such as certain administrative or technological activities. Concentrate on those roles in management development in which you maintain frequent contact with managers and on areas which are commonly experienced by managers as difficult. The experiences you gain will be beneficial for your future career. Avoid becoming a specialist in management development but develop transferable skills.

Maintain your network

Continue to communicate with those who are important for your return plan, even if you have no formal business issues to discuss. Make sure you always repeat the positive aspects of the management development function but emphasize its place in your career with the ultimate goal to become an all-round top executive. Remind your audience from time to time that the role is a temporary one. This will prevent others from speaking on your behalf and interpreting your enthusiasm: 'She appears to be very happy in this position, so she will probably want to continue in this field.'

Enter the arena

If you are convinced that you will not be happy or successful in the new role, consider refusing it. First, investigate if refusing an offer may have serious

consequences for the rest of your career. In some companies, the unwritten rule is that you can only once refuse a proposed function without negative consequences. In other companies, refusal may lead to the start of exit procedures.
Be prepared to accept the consequences if you take the route of refusal.

Choose the most appropriate way to communicate your decision to refuse the offer. Apart from delivering the message yourself in a meeting with the committee, you may consider asking a trustee from your network to convey the message. Avoid developing negative feelings about the process and learn to take it as a positive leadership challenge: how to turn a refusal into a career opportunity. After all, turning around negative situations is a skill line managers need to rely upon all the time when dealing with emotions of people in their teams. Your way of handling this situation will demonstrate your professionalism and at the same time give you the opportunity to bring forward convincingly your true ambitions.

Be prepared for any reaction, positive or negative, from the other party. Make sure you have done your homework by analyzing exactly the reasons why you were put forward for the role and which arguments were used. Continue to have a positive attitude toward the role itself but demonstrate with rational arguments and facts why you consider yourself to not be the most-qualified candidate. End the conversation with a statement about your long-term ambition and reinforce your commitment to stay with the company. It may be helpful to remember and share why you selected this company in the first place and what it has brought you to date.

Promotions

Your decision to accept a certain position at a company is determined by the opportunities offered and the possibility to realize personal growth. Alongside the working conditions and fringe benefits, the outlook of a career path is of crucial importance. In most industries career advancement first of all depends on acquiring the necessary technical knowledge and diplomas. The career path to the top may appear relatively straightforward and transparent. Often, there is an expectation that you will advance in predefined steps from junior to middle to senior positions. You will get your first promotion after a number of years, provided your performance is in accordance with the requirements (the rule of meritocracy). It is often clear which functions and paths will ultimately lead to top positions and which will most probably not. Nevertheless, women frequently report surprise that they are passed over for a promotion or senior role they expected to receive.

Why did I miss this promotion?

Description

An accounting and consultancy firm offers a well-defined career path. Every year a number of consultants are promoted to the next level. A female manager who has shown excellent performance during a number of years has reached middle management. Despite the continuance of her excellent performance she has been passed over a few times for a senior position. She notices that one of her colleagues, who only recently started working for the company and is less experienced, has been appointed to the senior role she aspired to. She wonders why she was passed over for this promotion again while she seemed to be the best-qualified candidate.

Analysis

Missing a promotion is an emotional event. After the initial disbelief, you may experience disappointment and anger. Women have a tendency to find fault with themselves, whereas men more frequently blame the circumstances and remain positive ('My time will come'). Although self-reflection and the ability to put things into perspective are excellent qualities for learning, they may well block personal growth if feelings of failure and self-blame prevail. This leads to stagnation and difficulties in continuing the journey.

A company is not a democracy in which employees have 'a right to promotion' if they objectively qualify for it. Apart from objective measures, other factors may be decisive in this process, such as those indicated in the pattern of power, performance, and promotion (see Chapter 3). At the start of their career most women concentrate on executing their tasks well and strive for more than 100 percent perfection. Dotting all the i's and crossing all the t's is the name of the game. This focus, however, can seriously undermine their delegation skills. After having been passed over for a promotion they suddenly realize that components other than performance should receive more attention. Through the delegation of executive tasks, more time can be allocated to developing powerful networks and paying attention to building a professional reputation. Instead of focusing on 'doing things right', in senior management you need to focus on 'doing the right things'. The difference between the two is commonly referred to as the difference between being a manager and being a leader. The way to the top is not about continuously working harder and harder, but about working smarter: delegating tasks and placing priority on building power networks and a professional reputation.

Strategies

New round, new chances

This round has not been successful, but there is always the next round of promotions. After analyzing the reasons for missing out this time, start positioning yourself for next year's round. Organizing a promotion is a skill that can be learned, so take up this new challenge as crucial learning in your leadership development process. It starts with attitude, so developing the winning attitude for the next round of promotions is a prerequisite for success.

Upgrade your performance

First, objectively analyze if your performance this time was up to standard. Assess if you have achieved all your goals according to plan and if reviews have been done properly. An excellent performance is a prerequisite for promotion.

Secondly, assess your compliance with the unwritten rules and informal performance requirements. These are more difficult to discover and to influence. Investigate which other colleagues did not receive a promotion despite their objective compliance with the performance targets and the reasons why, if possible. In addition, determine if the promoted colleagues outperformed their targets, achieved an extra goal, or delivered an extraordinary performance, for instance acquiring a new important client, solving a difficult issue, or publishing an article.

Thirdly, analyze your possibilities not only to achieve an excellent performance again but also to deliver an extra goal which might increase your chances of promotion in the next round. It is important to understand how to deliver the 'extras' needed for a promotion.

Formulate your ambition

The step to senior positions is reserved for the few, so you need a well-developed strategic plan to become one of them.

First, you need to gain understanding of the formalities and official procedures involved. Two parties are important to become acquainted with: the people responsible for putting forward candidates and the people responsible for the final decision. In addition, you need to be aware of people who can influence the process or decision but stand at the sidelines. This is the informal network that exercises substantial influence on important issues.

Make sure that you have an 'elevator pitch-like' speech, in which you bring forward your ambition to reach a senior position. This three-step approach may assist you:

1. In the first part you describe your core competencies and your achievements. For instance: 'I am an expert in connecting with people. Last year I brought in five new corporate clients, with an annual turnover of 500,000 euros. Two new colleagues have been brought in to handle the increase in turnover.

2. In the second part you elaborate on your long-term ambition connected to this short-term promotion. For instance: 'It is my ambition to be a director in five years' time and to contribute substantially to the development of our client portfolio in Asia. This promotion provides me with the opportunity to gain experience with managing effectively in different cultures.'

3. In the third part you indicate that you are already operating at the level you aspire to be promoted to. Focus on those elements of the new job that you feel you have mastered and act in accordance with your new role. Avoid drawing attention to those elements in the new role that you are less comfortable with. If you behave like you have made the promotion already, you will be seen as a more credible candidate than if you emphasize your (perceived) imperfections.

Make your ambition tangible and measurable by mentioning figures and concrete results if possible. Avoid emphasizing 'what you like' about the job and instead concentrate on how you will add value to the company should you be promoted. In order to be a contender for the next round of promotions you need to vocalize your ambition and skills with confidence and conviction. Because the process might involve many formal and informal interviews, your story needs to be consistent and repeated frequently.

Create a broad foundation

Having a broad foundation means that people with a say in the organization have a positive opinion about your capabilities and are willing to support you. This support is primarily based on competencies and results: your image of being a professional who is able to get things done. Creating a broad foundation for a promotion is a long-term strategy. As soon as you know who is responsible for proposing and deciding on candidates and who is influencing the process informally, you need to develop relationships with some of the key decision-makers. Develop these relationships carefully and on the basis of reciprocity. The trust built up in this informal network should be used only at crucial times, for instance when you need an extra vote of confidence or someone to put in a good word for you. The strength of your connections will be tested as soon as your name comes up for a promotion.

A common mistake is to rely on support from your subordinates. Some women have reported to be surprised that they missed out on a promotion despite the fact that they were very popular with their subordinates. Unfortunately, the backing of people who are not influential in the decision-making process is of little avail. There are many examples of women leaders who had broad support on the ground but were not promoted since they were not supported at top level. Although support on the ground is very important, support at other levels is often the decisive factor.

Develop your promotion competency

Your promotion capability is based on three pillars. The first pillar is your specialist *knowledge and experience*. Industry expertise, at both operational and strategic level, is indispensable. A thorough understanding of the development phase and the direction of the company and the industry sector are essential to determine in which fields the chances for promotions are the best. This also applies to your area of expertise. Insight into prevailing trends and developments in the mid- and long term will provide you with a broader view of potential opportunities for advancement. Systematically collecting information enables you to update your knowledge in timely fashion or make a career switch when the prospects in your industry have deteriorated. Timely reassessment of your possibilities ensures that your career continues to develop positively.

The second pillar consists of the *skills* that serve as tools for the efficient application of your knowledge and experience. Without excellent communication skills you will not be able to express your ambition eloquently or draw attention to your contributions to the company's results. The ability to delegate tasks and adapt to changing circumstances and cultures are as indispensable. All skills are part of your toolkit and enable you to respond effectively to any event on your way to the top. Women need an extra instrument in many organizations, such as the capability to operate in a male-dominated corporate culture. This requires openness and willingness to get to know this culture, and the flexibility to operate effectively in it. Not all women are prepared to adapt to a male-dominated culture. However, a professional might compare it with being an effective leader in a completely different country's culture. If you want to be successful as a leader in China, you prepare well in advance by trying to get to know the specificity of the culture and communicating with the people. A list of 'do's and don't's' should be part of the training process. Without a good understanding of the basic principles of Chinese society, chances for success are slim. Similarly, women in male-dominated cultures need to tap into their cultural sensitivity if they ever want to reach a top position.

The third pillar of your promotion competency is tied to the aspect of *timing*: choose the right timing and develop a proper plan. As in competitive sports, it is imperative to be at your best at the right moment in order to appear in the spotlight of the decision-makers. Reaching your peak too early or too late, or in an environment without the right people present, does not give you an advantage. Make sure to plan your peak moments carefully so you will benefit from the extra attention. The right timing starts with the right planning of the preparatory activities. Developing your goals and planning schedule is of extra importance for women because they are more likely to adapt their planning in order to fit with other goals, such as caring for children or the elderly, temporarily working part time or for other reasons. Although employment contracts and collective bargaining agreements cater for facilities and flexibility, the consequences for the individual woman are not neutral. In some corporate cultures people who work part time are considered to have insufficient commitment and ambition. In these cultures periods of working part time may have a negative effect on career advancement. Therefore, it is imperative that women (and men) consider the possible negative impact and actively shape the image around their ambition and commitment. It may well be that your perceived lack of ambition and commitment is interpreted by others that you have left the career track altogether. Actively communicating your ambitions remains crucial during periods of part-time work.

Good promotion planning takes into account the necessary shift in the allocation of time and effort from performance-related tasks to tasks related to policy and strategy, as described in Chapter 3 about the pattern of power, performance, and promotion. Your promotion competency relies on having support at crucial places when you are proposed as a candidate.

Create your coalition

No one reaches the top on their own. Investigate how effective leaders in your organization compose their teams. Often, they will invite the same people over and over again. Some people seem to move with the leader to the next promotion and onward. Especially when climbing the ranks it is essential to have trustworthy and reliable staff. Consider taking them with you to your next position. Many women qualify this behavior as unethical and detrimental to the company's interests. However, it is important to have your own team of people that you can trust when you reach a top position. Make sure that you have the final say in the composition of your team, especially when you have been recruited externally. Reconsider to accept people on your team who have been working with your predecessor and maintain good connections and feelings of loyalty to him or her.

Why do I not get the credit I deserve?

Description

A female member of a project team is responsible for a number of specific tasks in the project. Unfortunately, the project leader does not deliver on expectations and clearly lacks the ability to lead the team effectively. Team members complain about his detached management style and formal methods of communication. Gradually the female team member develops into the informal team leader. She becomes the spider in the web, ensures open communication between the members, creates the necessary connections in the team, and mediates in internal conflicts. At the same time she maintains the image to the outside world that the project leader is firmly taking charge of the project.

Her motives for assuming this role are simple: as a professional, she is keen to perform well even if she has to work harder or take on extra tasks. She fears that it would harm her reputation if the project failed.

Because of the female team leader's extra efforts the project is finally completed successfully. All project team members, including the leader, internally agree and acknowledge that her role has been decisive in achieving the good end result. During the official presentation of the project's results to the board, her crucial contribution is mentioned very briefly and the project leader receives all the praise.

A few weeks later she reads in the company's internal magazine that the project leader has been promoted to a very sought-after position. In the article, reference is made to the excellent results he achieved with the project. Since her career has not made any significant progress since the project ended, she feels undervalued and increasingly uncomfortable with the situation, and questions what she could have done differently.

Analysis

It appears that the female team member fulfilled the project leader's role without receiving the usual rewards, such as an official title, financial compensation, or another sign of appreciation, for example a mention in the company's internal magazine. If this was a test of her abilities to become project leader she certainly passed. However, her performance was only recognized among a small group of colleagues and was not officially on record.

From the case study it becomes clear that if you perform above expectations, you need to capitalize on this yourself. Public recognition will not automatically follow, so you need to be prepared to take action yourself. In some organizational cultures the project leader would have shared in public the excellent work done by the female team member, but in competitive cultures this would not be the case.

One of the most important characteristics of leaders is to create an inner connection (knowing your ambition and direction) and a connection with others (inspiring people to follow you). The value of this competency is clearly demonstrated in this case study. Experience shows that women in teams often take the role of liaison officer and informal leader. Even if some recognition for this role is expressed, it remains hidden and without consequence for their career.

Strategies

Declare your self-interest

If your role in a team gradually becomes more and more important for the project's completion, you should make it known in the organization before the project ends. The first step is to enter into negotiations with your underperforming team leader. If he or she understands the importance of your role, he or she will be keen to maintain the status quo. Analyze the extent to which your team leader exercises influence in the company and make an inventory of the networks he or she belongs to. Investigate what value he or she can add to your career advancement and how he or she could support you. Establish your preferred outcome in the negotiations and only keep your self-interest at heart this time.

Capitalize on the opportunity

Consider taking some of the following steps:

- Require the project leader to publicly acknowledge your role by appointing you officially as vice-chair, assistant project leader, or co-project leader. This will give you the advantage of having your hard work officially recognized in public and in your personnel file.
- If you would like to further develop your skills as a future project leader, negotiate to be allocated some of the formal leadership tasks during the project.
- Agree that if you continue in your role the project leader will support you in your endeavors to become team leader for the next phase of this project or a similar new project.
- Ask the project leader to write a letter of recommendation when you apply for a course at a top university or for entry to an important conference.
- Have the project leader introduce you to a person in the company who is important for your career.
- Suggest the project leader to put forward your name for a promotion or interesting assignment you have become aware of.

Unpopular and difficult tasks

Newcomers quickly discover the so-called 'difficult' assignments in an organization. They are the activities that attract very few or no volunteers. Difficult assignments have a high degree of complexity, which increases the chances of mistakes and failures. Other characteristics include unclear lines of command and the involvement of too many people of different disciplines and organizational entities. This absence of transparency in the command structure may lead to serious stagnation in decision-making since no one is truly responsible. It can also lead to lengthy multi-party meetings and even a need for mediation in order to reach a decision at all. Unpopular assignments often lack resources (staff) and, more importantly, budgetary and decision-making power. Some unpopular projects are characterized by a significant distance in hierarchy, as in the instance of a secretary who has been assigned to check the correctness of declarations of travel expenses from the directors and reports directly to the CFO about the findings. Unpopular tasks are often put forward with great enthusiasm and many times involve exaggerated praise for someone's skills for the job. Change-management roles are notorious for having no or limited resources or budget and lack of transparency in decision-making and lines of responsibility. Since change management usually involves radical shifts in responsibilities and tasks, people issues are the most sensitive to deal with, especially when you have no formal hierarchical power. These projects rely on a high degree of cooperation outside formal channels and goodwill.

Why do they often approach me for difficult tasks?

Description

A successful manager returns from maternity leave to discover that a few crucial decisions have been taken by the management team during her absence. One of the decisions relates to the transfer of a number of activities from her unit to another. She soon finds out that the activities left in her portfolio consist of the most challenging and unpopular ones. In addition, she is approached to take responsibility for the integration of two underperforming departments under her unit. She knows that a couple of managers had refused the project because they anticipated serious problems with employees and the works council. A year ago, the same project failed miserably and ended in a labor conflict with the project leader, who ultimately had to leave the company.

She feels very uncomfortable with the situation she is suddenly confronted with and questions why this is happening.

Analysis

Almost all jobs include a variety of less popular activities, but you need to prevent your name always being top of the list for difficult projects. If you are hardly ever assigned the most favored projects, you need to thoroughly investigate the reasons why. You may find that you are missing adequate and timely information and warning systems which protect you from these situations. You may not have communicated clearly about your skills and qualifications for other tasks, so people assume you like difficult assignments. You may actually have very specific and rare talents for solving difficult matters, which may serve you well if you know how to use them in your strategy for advancement.

Strategies

Turn it into a stretch assignment

Consider turning a difficult project into a 'stretch assignment'. Stretch assignments are tasks that require certain skills, experience, or knowledge which you might not have developed yet or which might not be part of your normal career path. These activities take you out of your comfort zone and require that you stretch yourself. This will build a positive reputation. The strategy to successfully turn an unpopular project into a stretch assignment depends on the following elements:

- Communicate widely the challenges of the assignment and the skills needed to complete it successfully. Document the seriousness of the situation, the impact it has on the company as a whole, the desired outcome of your intervention, and the competencies and planning to resolve it.

- Involve management and the HR department to assist you in translating the required competencies to the existing job structure. This exercise ensures that the weight of the role is not underestimated in terms of both financial compensation and recognition. Very often, stretch assignments are in fact a promotion because of their complexity and sensitivity.

- Negotiate an extra reward for completing the task. Since it is a challenging and difficult assignment for which normally no one volunteers, an extra reward is appropriate.

- Instead of, or in addition to an extra reward, consider negotiating enrolment onto a prestigious management course. This demonstrates that the stretch assignment is part of your strategic plan to develop into an all-round manager.

- Negotiate a specific time frame to complete the project. If you expect multiple problems, as in the case study, it is advisable to limit your assignment to, for instance, one or two years. This prevents you from being confined to a negative situation for too long.

- Organize your support and backup system. Communicate clearly about your expectations regarding management's involvement. Indicate how you plan to update management on progress and possible problems.

- Investigate who else besides the management team has an interest in the outcome of the project and demand introductions if necessary. Invest time to build up productive relationships with all stakeholders in the project.

- Agree upfront the way in which the company will communicate about the project. Consider involving the PR department to develop a professional communication plan, applicable to both success stories and unexpected calamities in the project. If possible, negotiate a final say in the texts published about the project.

- Prepare for an excellent execution of the assignment by analyzing potential pitfalls which may stand in the way of successful completion of the tasks. Organize mentors and coaches, inside and outside the company, to help you deal with these situations.

- Negotiate upfront signing authority and a budget for hiring external consultancy or mediation services. This will enable you to move quickly if needed.

- Develop an extra safety net in case your initial support and backup system fails. Due to the strategic importance of the assignment for your career, a direct relationship with one of the board members might prove to be essential for your future. This relationship will also protect you from negative publicity when the project enters a difficult phase.

Prevention tactics

To prevent difficult assignments landing on your desk, consider the following strategies:

- Be able to put forward names of alternative suitable candidates. This will help the selection committee in its task and provide an opportunity to enter into a serious discussion about criteria and qualifications for the assignment.

- Improve your image by more actively managing your competencies on the job.

- Make sure you stay connected to the company when you are on leave.

Board appointments

A growing number of organizations are looking for female board candidates. Stimulated by the explosive growth in private initiatives, requirements in corporate governance codes, and various law proposals for quotas, the demand for qualified female candidates has never been greater. On the other hand, the numbers of female board members are still increasing slowly.

In 2010 the percentage of women on the boards of Europe's largest listed companies in the 27 EU countries was 12 percent.[9] The number of female CEOs was 3 percent. The Scandinavian countries record significantly better scores than the rest of Europe. Norway has the highest score with 39 percent since the implementation of the 40 percent quota legislation. Sweden, Finland, and Denmark have achieved relatively high numbers (26, 26, and 18 percent respectively) without implementing quota legislation. The quota debate across Europe has a significant influence on the willingness of companies to actively seek female board candidates and to put policies in place to recruit and retain them.

How do I successfully land a board position?

Description

A female senior executive vice-president at an international bank, aspiring to be appointed to the next level, the executive board, has spent considerable time composing an impressive résumé upon request by an executive searcher. Despite the fact that her experience and credentials are top quality, she observes that some of her male colleagues, even those with lesser qualifications, achieve a non-executive board position fairly easily, whereas she fails even to be invited for interviews. Her regular visits to the executive search company to promote herself do not produce the desired result. Which strategies could she follow to increase her chances of being appointed to a board?

Analysis

The reasons why women are under-represented on boards are multiple and not unambiguous. In addition, the reasons manifest themselves at various levels: societal, company, and individual level. Some of the most frequently cited elements are:

- *Societal level*: preconceptions about the role of women; absence of female role models; (un)availability of facilities for care (children, elderly); impact of taxation.
- *Company level*: corporate culture; absence of women in informal networks; biased recruitment and promotion systems; over-representation in supporting roles; lack of women with line-management and expatriate experience.
- *Individual level*: individual career choices; work–life issues; resistance toward power and politics; insufficient visibility; ambivalence in ambition; peer pressures.

Strategies

Apart from waiting for quota legislation (such as in Norway) to stimulate demand, you can increase your chances of success significantly by developing appropriate strategies.[10] The proposed strategies primarily relate to board positions in medium to large companies, which are most visible. This does not devaluate in any way appointments to smaller companies' boards or non-commercial organizations.

Five-year plan

A successful strategy contains (at least) a five-year plan, depending on the level and relevance of your business experience to date. The five-year plan starts with the information phase, in which you learn about the content of the job ('what'), the general criteria you need to fulfill ('who'), and the route to secure a position ('how'). During the inventory search you will find large discrepancies between board positions in different companies. The criteria for board positions at a local or internationally listed company differ from those for start-ups, hospitals, non-governmental organizations, or building societies. Also the way candidates are recruited differs. Large, internationally listed companies primarily work through executive search companies or through networks of the current board members and management. On boards of start-ups there is often a relationship with the financiers.

Generally speaking, you need some 20 years of top-level experience to even be considered for a non-executive or supervisory board position. Based on your business experience and education you should determine the industry in which you can add real value. Consider taking additional or specialized courses that are relevant to your aspirations. It may not be very effective to enroll in a prestigious international board program if it is your intention to help a local start-up company.

Beware of flattery

Recent changes in local corporate governance codes and the implementation of legislation like the Sarbanes–Oxley Act have led to a significant increase in responsibility for board members.[11] Generally, more emphasis is placed on crucial elements of independence and expertise. Recent research in the United States has shown that it takes more than relevant experience and educational background for women to be appointed as a supervisory board member.[12] Our current system of identification and appointment of supervisors does not ensure the highest quality of corporate governance at all. The labor market for non-executives deviates fundamentally from the ideal of meritocracy, which strives to appoint 'the right person in the right place' in two aspects:

- Behavior aimed at monitoring and controlling risks is not rewarded although it is proven to have a positive effect on effective corporate governance, contrary to self-ingratiation behavior.
- Demographic minorities (women and ethnic minorities) receive fewer rewards for self-ingratiation behavior and are punished more severely for monitoring and controlling behaviors.

Flattery seems to be a more effective strategy to obtain a board position than demonstrating competencies crucial to the tasks of monitoring and controlling risks.

Above all, women who have mastered these competencies are punished more harshly for it than men. The system has a negative impact on the quality of corporate governance since it promotes board members who build their popularity more on flattery than on skills. In various discussions with supervisors across Europe many expect the outcomes of the American research to apply to their local situation, too. Women aspiring to a board position should be aware of the possible implications of this disparity in their individual situation.

Capitalize on the quota debate

The quota debate across Europe that started in Norway has led to a heightened attention for potential candidates. Make sure your ambition is known and actively attend events where current board members meet aspiring ones. Become an advocate and generate publicity for the cause and yourself.

Classic strategy: wait to be asked

The mechanism of the past, waiting to be asked, still works to a certain extent and in certain industries. Non-executive posts are still considered by many to be a position of honor and esteem given to former executive board members and their close relations in the business world. A prerequisite for this strategy is to be part of a network of strategically important contacts. Since very few women serve on executive boards or are part of the old boys' networks, this strategy generally has little chance of success for women.

Infiltrate the old boys' network?

Characteristics of the old boys' network are that it is closed to outsiders and that access is restricted through cooptation by its members. It is non-existent as an organization but very much alive in the public opinion, often in a negative way. For women, the old boys' network is difficult to infiltrate since it requires connections at top levels of organizations; very few women belong to those informal circuits.

Via the 'new girls' networks'?

In the past decade informal professional women's groups have emerged across industries and sectors, locally and trans-European. Its members meet regularly and actively exchange information about business developments. They are well connected to top levels in corporations and government, and are increasingly supporting and introducing each other for business opportunities and board positions. The informal character and relatively small numbers make the influence and impact of these 'new girls' networks' still limited.

In addition, many traditional women's networks have started initiatives around the advancement of women to board positions and are working with executive searchers and companies to identify and train potential candidates.[13] These networks serve as platforms for creating visibility for potential candidates and stimulating public debate about specific issues women encounter in the labor market. However, since most women's networks have very few members in top positions themselves, they present a less viable strategy to achieve a board position.

Route by way of executive search

The growing market for female board candidates undeniably has led to an increase in executive search companies specializing in this target market. It is well known that traditional executive search companies generally have to spend twice the amount of time and effort to find suitable female candidates. Undoubtedly this is related to the fact that traditional firms are led almost exclusively by men, who are used to searching for candidates primarily in their own networks. The increased demand from clients has prompted many firms to build a database of qualified female candidates. However, statistics show that this process has not produced a significant increase in women being appointed yet. Despite the large numbers of qualified female candidates in their databases, clients still seem to prefer selecting a male candidate.

If you decide to choose the route by way of an executive search company, the first step is to select one with a good track record in assignments in the industry in which you aspire to obtain a board position. Inquire about the number and frequency of their assignments in this industry and their track record of successful searches. Unfortunately, some have become champions in proposing female candidates without landing concrete appointments. A common misperception is that an executive searcher works for the candidate and looks after his or her best interests. It is important to realize that companies are their customers, pay for their services, and take the final decision to hire a candidate. The pressure on corporations to include female candidates in recruitment and selection procedures for board positions has become a real challenge for executive searchers. There is a risk of serious candidates being used by clients that have no real intention to actually appoint women and just want to demonstrate their efforts in trying to find them. When selecting an executive search firm you need to remain alert so as not to become one of its 'eternal' candidates instead of a much sought-after board member.

Create effective visibility

There are multiple ways of creating effective visibility. Good examples are starting up new initiatives and projects, writing articles for publication in professional magazines, and accepting a voluntary board position. The visibility attached should be related to the weight of the position you aspire to, as if you were promoting yourself as a future board member. If you pursue name recognition through media presence, your choice of media should be inspired by the media frequently used and trusted for its high quality of information by the target group.

Attending conferences and events, and memberships of clubs and networks take considerable amounts of time but help to create visibility, too. In your presentation and activities you need to keep in mind that your behavior will be assessed in light of your aspiration to become a board member.

Become active in voluntary organizations

Pursuance of leadership positions in voluntary organizations is an excellent strategy, provided it offers sufficient high-level contacts and opportunities to expand your current network. The level of professionalism in a voluntary organization might be lower than in business life. Therefore, activities may also take more time and effort to organize. A frequently heard complaint of board members of voluntary organizations is that only a few members carry their weight. It is advisable to agree to a time limit on the hours you can devote to the position and to your tenure in general. It is important to develop the ability to say 'no' in order to prevent gradually taking over more tasks from others, which is a common phenomenon. Choose consciously which voluntary organization you will contribute to based on its expected added value to implement your strategy.

Often, the most interesting volunteer board positions are not advertised but organized through informal connections. Find out which local interest groups or associations promote the interests of board members and directors, consider joining them, and become active. They provide you not only with the opportunity to expand your network, but also with the possibility to find mentors, learn from experienced board members, and discover additional routes to achieve your goal.

Accepting an unpaid board position at a charity or association although your ambition lies in the business world may seem a good strategy since 'you need your first board position to be approached for more'. Unfortunately, the reality is that a time-consuming volunteer board position in an organization which has few ties to your business community will prevent you from purposefully expanding your chances to reach your original goal. Although expanding your network into new sectors is interesting and intellectually stimulating, it may not be strategically efficient.

Private equity route

Not only for start-up companies but also for medium and large companies the demand for qualified board members on behalf of private investors, investment funds, or private equity companies has grown exponentially. This has resulted in an additional market which could be tapped into by women. Often, these companies have a database of candidates that they approach for specific roles. Since these parties primarily focus on financial gain (short term in dividends or long term through the sale of the company), they expect board members to have an expert background in finance.

Route through the works council

The articles of an organization may include the provision that a certain number of board candidates need to represent the employees. This is the case in Germany, Denmark, and Hungary. Currently, 23 percent of employee representatives on boards of Europe's largest companies are women, which is twice as high as the average (which stands at 12 percent).[14] The employee representative route has become a relatively successful one for women.

A variation on this rule is the provision that the works council has the right to propose (but not appoint) a board candidate on its behalf. It is advisable to investigate your country's regime and the viability of this route.

Route through education

Since it may well take five years before you attend your first meeting as a non-executive director, it is important to stay abreast of all developments in three key areas: corporate governance, director's liability, and financial reporting and strategy. Attending courses and seminars will keep your knowledge up to date and at the same time expand your network of relevant contacts. The explosive supply of training and courses give the impression that they are a requirement for a supervisory board position. Many women have taken expensive courses expecting that it will significantly increase their chances. Although permanent education is crucial for any aspiring board member, experienced board members indicate that relevant management experience is still valued higher than any course or seminar.

CHAPTER 9

Skills

9.1 Realizing your ambitions

Skills enable you to maneuver toward your goal. On the one hand, they are the link between your ambition and leadership statement ('What do you want to achieve and why?'). One the other hand, they are the various ways you shape your career within the parameters of the playing field ('How do you reach your goal?'). Ideas and intentions are useless without the essential leadership skills to, for instance, effectively communicate and negotiate within the frames of power and politics.

In this chapter the following FAQs are addressed:

- Why do I not receive what I am asking for?
- Why do I get remarks about my appearance?
- How do I promote myself without provoking resistance?

9.2 FAQs

Any negotiation process revolves around certain limits set by the parties involved. How much is one willing to give in order to improve one's own position? It is a game of winning and losing arguments until you reach agreement. One of the most challenging negotiations for women is around salary and working conditions. Across Europe women on average earn 17.8 percent (2008) less than men for the same work.[1]

In most cases a new recruit has an information discrepancy regarding the organization and the negotiation process. How do you make sure that you get what you ask for and, more importantly, that you know what to ask for in the first place?

Why do I not receive what I am asking for?

Description

A female account manager at an insurance company enters into negotiations on her appointment. Next to the usual salary and benefit packages on offer, she needs to agree on the composition of the client portfolio the company presents her with. It is customary at the company to guarantee new recruits in their first year in office a certain income from the allocated client portfolio. This enables the account manager to learn the ropes and get acquainted with the company's products and sales structure. During the negotiations about the composition of the portfolio she questions the low number of good-quality clients and consequently the rather low guarantee amount. It appears that a sizeable amount of her allocated clients have been performing badly over the past years. Arguing this fact, she refuses the company's proposal and puts forward a higher guarantee amount. Her proposal is immediately turned down: 'Our offer is our standard arrangement for all new account managers. What you are asking for is not acceptable.' In the end she believes the arguments of her negotiating partner and accepts the offer; after all, she has no reason to doubt her future colleagues' honesty.

A few years later she has developed an excellent reputation in the company. She has been approached to take part in a task force with the mandate to review the recruitment procedures for new account managers. By coincidence she hears from one of the task force members that he received a different package than she had at her appointment. During the work of the task force it becomes clear that almost 40 percent of new account managers deviated from the standard and negotiated a better package. She wonders why she did not get what she asked for at the time. Why had she not been successful in being the exception to the rule like apparently so many others?

Analysis

It is possible that the case occurs structurally in the company, which indicates that there is a serious problem with the integrity of managers and their attitude toward negotiations with those who are less familiar with the company's culture. Discrimination in labor contracts is legally prohibited. If almost half of the new recruits receive a different package than the standard agreement, chances are that new recruits who rely on the integrity and honesty of the negotiators seriously lose out. As demonstrated by the macro-economic facts of the equal pay gap, this happens more often to women than to men. Next to differences in salary, the same effect can be observed in negotiations about promotions, content of the job, bonuses, enrolment courses, reimbursement of tuition fees, and other benefits. Research in the UK found that women working full time in the financial services sector received 55 percent less pay and a shocking 80 percent less bonus (performance-related pay) than their male counterparts.[2]

Various factors may cause women in general to be less effective in negotiations. First, not all women openly discuss with others issues to do with salary, other financial benefits, or the financial impact of the composition of their client portfolio, as in this case study. This may cause a serious lack of information on these topics, which leads to an early acceptance of the offer on the table.

Another factor is of a more social nature. When negotiations proceed, arguments and tone harden. Skilled negotiators create a climate which leaves no room for modesty. Some women respond to this by mentally withdrawing and accepting the offer too quickly out of fear of being labeled 'aggressive' or 'not so nice'. This is called the female modesty effect.[3] Unfortunately, they fail to realize that agreeing too quickly might lead to the other party losing respect for them and even questioning if they have selected the right person for the job. Research[4] has found that women managers have a different attitude toward negotiations than male managers and they feel less confident and satisfied with the result. Interestingly, there were no significant differences in the outcomes achieved between male and female managers.

Another factor that possibly causes a discrepancy is that women generally value the content of the function and the opportunities for self-development more than financial rewards and status of the job. When salary levels are transparent and standardized, little or no pay gap between men and women is reported. Discrepancies primarily appear in the 'extras' outside of the standard packages. Men sooner feel entitled to extras than women and, consequently, continue the negotiation process for longer, increasing their chances of success.

A last element of importance may be the natural inclination of many women to come to the point quicker in meetings. They take less time for the political bargaining process of give and take. Managers have reported that salary negotiations with male employees may take twice as long because they continue to put new offers and ideas on the table, whereas women just want to get on with business.

Regarding the case at hand, negotiations failed because the account manager had not prepared well for them. Without having done your homework, achieving a good result depends largely on the goodwill and fairness of your negotiation partner. You literally put your fate in their hands. Not only may this cause you to lose money, but it may also cause a psychological scar when you later discover you have been treated unfairly. If this happens again later, many choose to leave the company because of lack of recognition and reward. This is one of the causes of the vanishing act of women on their way to the top.

Companies that are serious about advancing women to senior positions take action to prevent this phenomenon from happening by reviewing and restructuring the negotiation process. If the process does not ensure equal outcomes, chances are that prejudices dictate its unequal outcome.

Strategies

Investigate your attitude

Negotiation skills can be developed and learned, so it is recommended you enroll on specialized courses in order to be better prepared. Since corporate and industry cultures pervade the negotiation process, it is wise to choose a training course that takes into account the special traits of the culture you are operating in. Special attention needs to be given to your attitude and possible frames which limit your negotiation strategy from the start. Some socially induced frames prescribe that women have indeed less right to the highest possible salary than men.[5] If you consciously or unconsciously accept this social norm, your attitude and expectation of the outcome of the negotiation will be affected in a negative way. Start the negotiations with a sense of entitlement to the highest salary and build your case around it.

Find mentors and coaches

Mentors and coaches are excellent tools to support you in the process of negotiating by helping you to develop your strategy and watch out for pitfalls on your side and the other. Mentors and coaches that have hands-on experience with negotiations in your industry, especially, can provide useful information about important negotiation practices.

Negotiate as agent instead of principal

Some women have reported being excellent negotiators about organizational issues but not when it comes to their own career and salary. They feel uneasy when they have to declare their 'monetary worth'. If you are not comfortable with tough negotiations, consider the strategy to negotiate on behalf of someone else, for instance on behalf of your team. Start by putting yourself in the shoes of your team and articulate the value of your contributions. Selling 'your skills' might be more comfortable than 'selling yourself'. Adopt this train of thought as the guideline for your salary negotiations and you may find it easier to strive for the maximum result.

Engage in benchmarking

Good preparation requires collecting information about similar employment contracts in the labor market. This gives a good indication of 'your monetary worth'. Use your informal networks to establish benchmarks for the result you should be able to negotiate. Be aware of the risk of comparing packages of female colleagues because women on average earn less than men and their packages will in general be less favorable. Include salary packages of male counterparts to prevent entering the negotiations with a lower level of expectation than they would. Benchmarking is only useful if you make sure gender differences are excluded.

Use salami tactics

The effectiveness of this technique depends on careful planning and execution. After establishing your desired end result you split up the total package into smaller pieces. By taking the time to negotiate every element separately, the negotiation process will take longer than when the complete package is on the table. A prerequisite for success is knowledge about the maximum you can achieve for each piece through careful preparation and benchmarking. Decide which elements have the highest priority and which are 'extras', and use the extras to avoid having to make concessions on your priorities. In addition, apply the technique of asking for too much at the start – around 30 percent more than your desired goal.

Negotiate as if you were a professional negotiator

Treat the salary negotiations as your professional job. See your counterparts as potential clients or suppliers who you want to impress with your professionalism and excellent negotiation skills. Remember that if you negotiate well for yourself, you only gain respect from your counterparts. If you fail to go for the maximum, your counterparts may wonder if they should have hired you in the first place.

For any strategy to be successful you need to start with the right attitude (sense of entitlement to the best result) and the willingness to be labeled 'not so nice' rather than 'incompetent'.

It's not all about appearance

Generally speaking, business women pay more attention to their looks and how others perceive them than men. Not only in dress but also in conduct and behavior women seem to be very conscious of the importance of making a good impression as a professional. Remarks about appearances are therefore often taken very seriously. The following case studies contain a few (extreme) examples of daily situations and proposed strategies to effectively deal with similar remarks.

Why do I get remarks about my appearance?

Description 1

A female senior manager at an international bank was standing in the elevator on her way to a business meeting. When the elevator halted at one of the floors, a group of men in dark gray suits entered and blended in with the group of identically dressed colleagues. Since the woman was dressed in a purple jacket and leather skirt she immediately drew the attention of one of the men. He looked her up and down, and again, his eyes focused on her purple jacket, when he said loudly for everyone to hear: 'Well well, aren't *you* brave!' There was a sudden hush in the elevator and all eyes were upon her. Many reactions went through her head, from anger and irritation to surprise about the silliness of the remark. Which reaction would be the best she wondered?

Description 2

Even more shocking are remarks about certain parts of the body. An extreme example is of a manager waiting in front of the door of the office of a director she had an appointment with. The door was open but since he was on the phone, she and her team remained waiting outside. When the director had hung up the phone, they entered the room. With a tone of surprise in his voice, he welcomed her: 'Oh, you were there already? I did not recognize you from your calves behind. Do you play field hockey, too?' The latter remark referred to a common joke among men that women who played field hockey had muscular, hairy legs.

Analysis

Both case studies are clear examples of macho behavior and power talk in front of a group of peers. Many women internalize remarks like these about their dress, behavior, and body. The urge to be liked can seriously hinder a spontaneous and adequate reaction in such a situation. Another common reflex is to start apologizing at the moment someone points out that your clothing deviates from the standard pattern. Some may actually feel that the jacket is indeed too purple and that it was a bad choice for the day.

A less effective reaction would be to take the criticism seriously and utter an apology or remain silent altogether while your face turns red. Such an admission of guilt over something which is not linked to your professional skills is a sign of insecurity. In many organizational cultures this reaction does not instill any respect.

In the second case study, is this type of remark acceptable at all? In strong assimilation cultures you are at risk of being labeled 'oversensitive' and 'not much of a sport' if you respond seriously or with a reprimand. As long as these types of rude remarks are made by one specific person or very incidentally, this person may well be the exception to the rule. But when similar remarks reflect the way women are being treated, the company has a major problem. Other indicators of culture problems are a greater outflow and under-representation of women in decision-making functions.

Strategies

Spontaneous emotional reactions, such as ignoring the issue, becoming angry or sneering, should be prevented since they will only evoke laughter from the audience. A better strategy is to regain control over the situation.

Mirroring

Instead of explaining why the remarks are testimony of bad taste, you give the speaker the same experience you just had. In the first case study you can apply this strategy easily. After the speaker says loudly for everyone to hear: 'Well well, aren't *you* brave!', you first look him in the eye, then up and down from his head to his toes, rest your eyes on his undoubtedly very dull neck tie, look him in the eye again and say firmly: 'Obviously you're not!' Often bystanders see the humor of the situation and start laughing. In very conservative circles you will be stared at by the audience since it is not expected that a woman responds at all, let alone puts the speaker in his place.

Deflection strategy

Another method is to accept the intimidating remark as if it were a compliment, and thereby weaken the implicit reproach or accusation. If you answer with a beautiful smile and clear voice 'How nice of you to say so!', demonstrating openness and goodwill in your posture, you will gain immediate respect of the bystanders. By elegantly including the audience through eye contact, the speaker's behavior may well become the topic of the discussion and not you.

Flying low or taking charge

More serious are situations like the second case study since they can evolve into excessive personal attention that makes you very uncomfortable or even harassed. Especially when derogatory remarks are made by potential or existing clients it is difficult to choose the correct response. You risk losing a client or alienating a prospect with serious consequences to your career. Remaining silent and refraining from taking action is a blow to your personal integrity. In the long term this may harm your sense of self-worth and self-confidence. Being the victim of someone else's bad behavior is unfair but fairly realistic too in many corporate cultures.

If you decide to take action you will need to be prepared to ultimately leave the company if you receive no support, since your career will be over by then. If you are not willing to accept the ultimate consequence, it is advisable to fly under the radar screen and abandon any plans for action. Consider carefully which way is best to bring the case to the attention of your company. It is likely that your line manager will suffer any consequences too because the client may become angry and withdraw his business. Next to your career, your manager's career may be harmed by this too. If you are not sure your manager will support you, and perhaps may even take it as an opportunity to move you from a project or your job, it is advisable to invite preferably a high-level trusted person to your first meeting with your manager. Prepare your case well and make sure you communicate a consistent and clear message. Express your concern that others in the company possibly have had or will have similar experiences with this client. Rely on the workings of your informal network to gather support for your case. Present the case as a test case for your company's senior management to convey the message that certain types of behavior are not tolerated, not even from clients. Refrain from making it personal and emotional since this is a business issue. Place the case in the broader perspective of the desired corporate culture based on integrity and respect. End the conversation by expressing confidence in the ability of the company's management to take appropriate actions. Maintain confidentiality about the event and the conversation, and continue working as before.

If this careful strategy does not lead to results and your career suffers, you probably are better off leaving the company and selecting an employer that values integrity and professionalism. If management takes action, you have learned a valuable lesson in leadership, which is to turn a 'no-win' situation into an advantage. In addition, you have played a major role in the development of the corporate culture, which is beneficial to all employees.

Self-promotion is a skill

Self-promotion is the skill to manage the impression others have about your competencies and character. Your professional image depends on subjective judgments from people in your business environment, from colleagues, clients, managers, and subordinates. Your conduct and speech contribute to their perception of you. If your image is not in line with your real intentions and qualities, remember that often 'perception is reality'. The ability to adequately promote yourself is an essential communication skill that becomes more important as the journey along the road to the top progresses, as is demonstrated in the pattern of power, performance, and promotion (Chapter 3). Since high turnover in managerial ranks has become a fact of life, you no longer can rely on your company's memory of your value. Therefore, promotion skills have become even more important. The key question to ask yourself is 'how can I put myself forward without putting others off?'

How do I promote myself without provoking resistance?

Description

A female senior director of an international transportation company has developed a serious reluctance to give interviews to the press. She claims interviewers are more interested in her answers to the eternal question 'how do you manage in such a male-dominated business?' than in the strategy and results of her company. In addition, her colleagues have expressed irritation about the content of her interviews in the past, which were a reflection of this line of questioning. Therefore, she decided to put forward the PR director and her other directors to give press conferences and interviews about achievements, successful projects, and events. She is convinced that they are better qualified than her to promote the business in the right way.

Serious changes in the logistics and transportation business prompt a number of major transportation companies to cooperate in a newly established federation. Alongside the aim of sharing knowledge and experiences with the upcoming changes in the environment, the group cooperates to exercise influence on pending legislation at government level. A joint committee is established with the ministry of logistics, representatives of political parties, and a few directors of transportation companies. The female director is confronted with the official launch of the committee when it is announced on the television news. She quickly assesses that the committee consists of a few competitors that have far less experience and respect in the community than she has. She realizes that they took her place and that she is missing out on an important opportunity for her future career. How could she have promoted herself better under these circumstances?

Analysis

Visibility is an issue of strategic importance: do you want to be visible in the first place, when do you want to create visibility, where, and with what message? In this case study the female director had built an excellent reputation inside her company but was less well known outside. It normally is very wise to leave a media campaign and public relations to specialists and experts. However, if this leads to a lack of name recognition for your own work, the strategy is counterproductive. Unknown, unloved.

The reason for the director's reliance on PR specialists came from the negative reactions she received in the past when she promoted herself. It is clear that the way she went about putting herself forward for interviews resulted in putting her colleagues off. In order to maintain good working relationships, her solution was to withdraw from the public limelight and rely on professionals in the future.

The impact of the strategy followed in this case study has negative consequences at several levels. First, the director feels passed over and undervalued although the result was a direct consequence of her chosen strategy. In addition, it deprives her from an excellent opportunity to build a network in high places in government and politics, which may benefit her in her career. Consequently, the company suffers from the fact that it will not be represented at the committee. It will therefore not have the possibility to influence the decision-making process around new legislation, nor will it benefit from having access to new networks of contacts and new information the others will have. In the end, the whole situation may therefore harm the company's competitive position.

It is a challenge to promote yourself without being suspected of doing so out of self-interest only. In the workshops women frequently expressed experiencing a dilemma because self-promotion does not feel natural and often evokes negative reactions in their environment. Therefore, they often prefer operating behind the scenes and relying on the workings of meritocracy ('I will be noticed automatically if I do my best') and the goodwill of others who are willing to promote them. Leaving your visibility to others is not a good strategy in a labor market with an ample supply of talent and an always limited supply of interesting and senior positions. Therefore, it is important to develop a toolkit of strategic communication skills.

Strategies

Google yourself

Research among international board members in Europe has shown that one out of three female board members does not have a public profile on Google.[6] This is in sharp contrast to the dozens of pages available on their male counterparts referring to articles, interviews, and information on companies' websites. The first step in promoting yourself is to Google your name and to review the information available about you. Does your public profile match the image you strive for? Remember that nowadays information on the Internet is widely used and often considered 'true'.

Go for effective visibility

Make sure that you are visible in relation to your goals. If your ambition is to achieve a senior management position but your public profile only shows pictures of you pouring chocolate milk at the local tennis tournament, next to your holiday snapshots, you need a strategic plan to increase your professional public image.

Identify the gap between your desired and perceived professional image

Develop your desired professional image. This consists of a description of the competencies and character traits you want other professionals to associate with you. These could be credibility, trustworthiness, reliability, business savvy, political prowess, empathic, inspirational, and result-oriented, to name a few. At the same time reflect on which traits you specifically do not want to be associated with. For instance, some are comfortable with emphasizing their role in the family ('first of all mother'), whereas others prefer to focus on their professional life.

Find out what image you currently have by speaking to your supervisors, subordinates, and trusted mentors. Comparing your desired and your perceived image provides you with essential information to bridge the gap.

Don't brag but contribute

Before you can effectively sell your message, you will first have to sell yourself. Bragging generally puts people off, but by making positive and professional contributions to a conversation you will improve your professional image. Excellent self-promoters know how to package their added value in stories and anecdotes and choose the right timing to make these interventions.

Seize chances to present yourself

Ask a question, give a speech, or enter a debate every time the opportunity presents itself. This will help you to conquer any fears of speaking in public and improve your self-confidence in the long term. Don't restrict this to business opportunities but test yourself also on private parties and events. Remember that you already gain respect for having the courage to speak up in the first place.

Create a 'less is more' statement

One of the standard storylines in the toolkit of communication skills is the famous elevator pitch – a 30- or 60-second commercial about yourself. Instead of calling it the elevator pitch, rephrase it into a 'less is more' statement. This contains the key elements of who you are and what you do, what you are passionate about, your added value and achievements for the company, and your ambition for the future. The statement ends with a question or invitation immediately linked to your goal for presenting yourself in that situation. The general aim is that the audience becomes interested in you and wants to hear more. An effective pitch is not a sales pitch or a short version of your résumé, but an engaging, interesting, and enthusiastic story which is inviting and inspiring. If you are not excited about yourself, who else will be? There are many situations in which you may unexpectedly find yourself in the presence of someone who might have the right connections, job, or information for your career advancement. One of the most frequently asked questions in my workshops was how to capitalize on those situations. This requires being able to quickly introduce yourself and create a connection. Take time to develop a pitch and use your leadership statement (Chapter 2) as a guideline. Practicing your pitch will ensure it comes naturally at the crucial moment.

Adapt your storyline

Always adapt your story to the needs of the audience. By taking into account the organizational culture and social structure you prevent your self-promotion creating fierce resistance. Your introduction to a group of corporate board members should contain elements of interest to them, such as relevant board experience and results you take responsibility for. After all, the goal of your speech is to create credibility as a future board member. Take the time to introduce yourself and resist any feelings of modesty when talking about your achievements so far.

Interestingly, when you use the same strategy and wording for your introduction to a group of female managers, it is possible that they feel uncomfortable. They are generally not used to a woman positioning herself so firmly and confidently. To prevent this resistance you can either adapt your story to their expectations or enter into a discussion about the phenomenon itself: reflecting on frames and prejudices and how they can hinder promoting yourself as you would like to be seen. The choice depends on your desired outcome of the meeting.

CHAPTER 10

Strategic Networking

10.1 Do women network differently?

The activity of strategic networking becomes increasingly important as your responsibilities on your way to the top increase in accordance with the pattern of power, performance, and promotion (Chapter 3). The type of networks you belong to evolves too, from formal and operational networks at junior level to informal and strategic networks at top level. As previous case studies have shown, being unknown in networks may lead to crucial information being missed. Many of the FAQs in this chapter therefore relate to building up and using networks, and networking as a strategic skill. The following issues will be addressed:

- Why is networking so important?
- Why am I always the last one to know?
- Why am I losing good clients to colleagues?
- How do I build a strategic network?

Networking is an investment in social relationships. All contacts, both in personal and in professional life, theoretically belong to your networks when you distribute information or support each other, provide advice, or just have a listening ear. A network is a collection of contacts linked through a common characteristic such as values (religious or community values), vision (lobby groups), ideas (inventors' network), hobby (music), or joint activities such as trade (companies) or the exchange of information or sharing of experiences (associations). Networks can be formalized in a legal structure or informal. Another dimension relating to networks is that some are of a personal nature (they include family and friends) and some are of a professional nature. Another distinction can be made between networks within a company and outside (other companies and industries).

The most important practical functions of networks in the professional field are as follows:

- They provide extra channels for relevant information outside formal channels
- They are the basis of so-called staying power (see 7.4)
- They provide access to the most favored and top positions
- They act as channels of strategic political play
- They are instruments in creating visibility and name recognition
- They are tools for 'getting things done'.

The great advantage of informal networks over formal hierarchical networks is the speed with which business can be done. One of the very few documented examples in the corporate world is the financing arrangement for Vivendi.[1] In 2002 this French telecommunications company needed a capital injection of three billion euros in just three days. Vivendi's CEO contacted his buddy group of rugby-loving CEOs, among which was the CEO of the insurance company AXA. He provided the capital within three days.

Indicators of an ineffective network can be:

- Difficulty in accessing leadership positions and high-profile roles
- Insufficient resources (budget, personnel)
- Exclusion from decision-making
- Insufficient support for proposals
- Underpayment and undervaluation
- Invisibility or lack of promotion of professional image
- Missing crucial information.

Culturally defined

The importance of building a network of contacts differs between cultures. In Asia *guanxi* is essential for doing business. Guanxi is the network of personal relationships which determine the extent of your influence. Guanxi is more than social capital since it requires a basis of loyalty and trust between the connections, which is stronger than any formal rank or hierarchy. The built-up personal trust can surpass the reputation of the company you work for or the quality of the product you sell. The workings of guanxi may force you to accept an inferior product delivered by your trusted connection even if better products are on the market. Guanxi may also compel a CEO to appoint a niece or nephew of the largest shareholder on the board of the company instead of recruiting and selecting the best candidate through regular procedures.

A characteristic of guanxi is that it is reciprocal and the relationship lasts forever if maintained properly. In the Western business world we have become used to shorter-term and less personalized relationships. Nevertheless, elements of guanxi can be found in our society too, for instance in the famous old boys' networks, in some alumni clubs of universities and schools, and in nobility and royalty.

Do women network differently?

Women in general rely more on 'what' they know than 'who' they know. Knowledge surpasses relationships. Networks, or social capital, can be divided into hard social capital and soft social capital.[2] Women's networks are traditional examples of soft social capital because they have a strong social–emotional function and provide safe environments to develop skills. Men are more concentrated on building hard social capital, based on experiences in business relationships. These networks provide career advice, coaching, connections, protection (such as staying power), and access to interesting positions. As women's careers advance from specialist to more generalist strategic roles, their need to build up efficient hard social capital increases. The information flow through the informal networks enables them to keep abreast of developments and influence the decision-making processes at an early stage. The ability to exchange knowledge and contacts and to communicate with various stakeholders about the future of the company is an essential trait of effective leaders.

A frequently observed pattern among women is that they tend to rely on only one manager for appreciation, feedback, and career advancement. However, when the manager leaves or the relationship gets strained, they may find themselves in a very vulnerable position. This is another reason for women to expand their informal networks and create trust relationships outside their hierarchical lines.

The share of female members of many directors' and official managers' clubs is generally very low. On the other hand, women are very active on the Internet through LinkedIn memberships. More than 40 percent of LinkedIn members are female. The advantage of online networking is the speed, the diversity of connection, and the information distributed via these channels. Online networks are motors of innovation and change since they connect across the world, industries, and functionalities.

10.2 How to build a strategic network

The ability to build strategic networks of relevant contacts becomes increasingly important during your career. As shown in Chapter 3 this skill may well be the decisive factor for reaching a top position. Building a strategic network takes ten concrete steps.

Step 1: Make an inventory of your network

Split the internal (such as your company's) from the external networks. Describe for each relationship its origin, being personal (P) or business (B). The origin may be an introduction by someone, a location, a conference, an event or a club, or travel (flight or hotel). Indicate what value you have added to this contact and vice versa. The value may lie in the future.

Your relationships can add value to your career in numerous ways, for example:

- They can provide relevant information (about competitors, markets, products)
- They can offer advice (career, personal, business)
- They can provide introductions (business and government connections, networks, associations, politics, etc.)
- They can provide skills and specific expertise (such as information about financial engineering, PR, marketing)
- They can increase the number of clients (potential clients, leads, new clients)
- They can provide valuable feedback (about your performance, image, presentation)
- They can offer moral support (in the case of a business conflict or personal tragedy)
- They can offer opportunities for cooperation (joint projects or business ventures)
- They can provide access to human resources (such as candidates for jobs or ventures)
- They can offer a mentoring or coaching relationship (in the role of mentor or mentee, coach or coached) – and so on.

It is useful to systematically review your contacts list and capture their (potential) value added in a schedule such as that at Table 10.1.

TABLE 10.1 Network inventory			
Name of contact (P, B)	Origin	Your added value	Contact's added value
Mr X (B)	*Previous manager of former company*	Helping out with difficult assignments	**Mentor (on topic of management skills)**
Mrs Y (B)	*Colleague in current management team*	Career advice at transfer (salary negotiations)	**Information on financial market**
Mrs Z (P)	*Colleague and school board member*	Moral support with raising difficult child	**Expertise on PR**

This exercise will immediately show if you have sufficient information available about people you meet. This will help you to focus more on collecting really useful strategic information next time you are networking.

Step 2: Identify the gap

After assessing the value of your current network, you need to develop a strategy for expanding your networks in the direction you have chosen. The expansion is built on the answers to the following questions:

- Where do I want to be in five years' time?
- What do I need in terms of education, experience, and connections?
- Do I currently have access to the networks of importance to realize my goal?

It is not important that everybody knows you and that you are part of every network, but those crucial for your plan should. Since your plan will evolve, step 2 should be repeated regularly.

Step 3: Identify the networks

Find out which people, organizations, and networks provide the best chances of meeting people who can help you realize your next ambition. Strategic career planning takes into account unexpected events such as reorganizations and even bankruptcy of a company or sector. Build your network as broad as possible so you always have connections in other industries if you decide to start a completely new career.

If you aspire to become the chief financial officer (CFO) of a company, it is useful to become a member of a professional organization of CFOs, accountants, or financial experts. If it is your ambition to take the role of CEO, more general business networks might provide good opportunities.

If you consider switching careers in a few years, identify networks in the field you are planning to move into. They will provide you with information about the sector and useful contacts.

Alumni networks of universities, business schools, and former employers are useful networks to maintain. The quality of an alumni network should even be one of the key criteria to select a course.

Women's networks can fulfill a role, too. It is a generation ago that women's networks primarily brought together politically engaged women to jointly address inequality and strive for emancipation. In the past few years organizations of professional women in corporate and government positions have developed. Their main goal is to provide a platform for women to meet and learn from each other. In addition, these networks offer a wide range of business activities and events aimed at developing managerial skills. Mentoring programs and inspirational role model sessions contribute to a positive learning atmosphere. The most advanced networks offer an online meeting place, with job fora, message boards, chat rooms, and communities to enable the search for new jobs, business partners, or clients. Companies that take leadership development for women seriously often implement a women's network as one of the tools to accelerate the process.

Step 4: Integrate into the network

Some people have a natural flair to connect with anyone in an unknown environment. Others need more time and preparation. In fact every activity, such as a conference, a job market, a reception, and an invitation to a hospitality room at a concert or sports event, is a networking opportunity. A good preparation consists of:

- Finding out or asking for a list of guests or members so you can select interesting connections beforehand
- Deciding which people you would like to meet and why, and carrying out your plan
- Searching for the network on the Internet and reading about the members and events
- Finding information about the board members and other key people in order to discover any previous connections or acquaintances you share

- Visiting the website and studying photos of events to get an impression of the activities
- Preparing a short opening story about yourself which relates to the theme of the network or event you are about to attend
- Concentrating on and being serious about networking, but staying relaxed in the process
- Enjoying the event, even if the event itself does not really interest you at all.

Do I really need to take up golf?

Some women prefer networking with other women over networking with men. The feeling of not belonging and being addressed as a waitress is reported frequently. This may prevent you from participating in events and visiting occasions which are important for business. How to blend in naturally is a skill that can be learned. It requires courage and perseverance alongside a strategic plan to make an uninteresting event worthwhile to you. If the network is worthwhile for your career, don't restrain yourself or deny yourself the opportunities presented. Select three people you want to meet for a purpose and execute your plan meticulously. Give yourself permission to only leave the occasion after completion of your task. Through this strategic approach an uninteresting event turns into a challenge to expand your network with high-value contacts, which will help your career.

If you don't like golf but from your research the golf club appears to be the best place to meet relevant people for your strategic plans, consider joining anyway and concentrate on those activities that you find interesting.

Presence counts

Make sure that people know that you attended the occasion and what your contribution was. It is recommended to ask questions or give an opinion when you attend an event for the first time. Since you can only make a first impression once, prepare which questions to ask and how to best present yourself. It is difficult to change perceptions, so it is imperative to give the members the impression that you joined the network for a business purpose. If your goal is to become a credible board member in a network consisting of board members, your interventions should be in line with your aspirations.

Go for power

If possible, become active on the board or committee of the organization. This will give you extra visibility and the opportunity to promote your qualities. Refrain from accepting positions that reinforce traditional female roles, hold lower status (like secretarial roles), or take a considerable amount of time, and from accepting routine work (such as producing name tags or guest lists). Avoid responsibilities that might take you away from networking during an event. A frequently observed pattern is that women assume responsibility for the catering and logistics. These tasks may cause frequent interruptions in important conversations during the event; this is not in your interest. The role of (vice) president or chair or another strategic role (e.g. finance or strategy) will not only you enhance your status , it gives you the opportunity to practice and develop certain leadership skills. A network is a relatively safe environment for testing your future leadership role.

Step 5: Networking **is** working

Networking is often seen as an extra task that has to compete in your busy life with other important activities related to work, family, friends, sports, education, and relaxation. Since it takes time before networking really pays off it is often not high on the list of priorities. This will change as soon as the benefits of networking become apparent. It requires a change in mindset that networking is a professional activity next to other professional activities such as attending meetings, drafting reports, and giving feedback to subordinates. The time allocated to strategic networking should therefore be included in your regular work time schedule. Time can be created by shifting time devoted to executive tasks through mastering the skill of delegation. This ensures that networking does not add to the burden but becomes an integral part of work. Effective networkers have excellent delegation and management skills. Deciding to make strategic networking part of your daily activities forces you to develop these skills further. In addition, the mindset will influence delegation of tasks at the home front. After all, 'having a drink with colleagues' has a less serious ring to it than 'attending a strategic networking event to meet X, Y, and Z who can help you with the next step in your career'.

Step 6: Invest wisely

Financial contributions vary substantially, so invest your time and money wisely and do a proper due diligence before joining a network, association, or club. The following strategies might be considered, especially when you are on a low budget:

- Get an introduction as a guest to attend your first meeting, in order to find out if the network is useful for you.
- Contact a current member to receive more information and possibly an introduction.
- Ask for a reduction or a waiver of the administration or introduction fee, if applicable.
- Investigate when the network organizes activities to recruit new members. Often, these activities include a temporary waiver of membership fees or first-time administration costs. Some networks give discounts if you are member of another network or alumni organization.
- Join free networks such as alumni networks of companies or universities, Chambers of Commerce, and online networks (e.g. LinkedIn).

Since networking is a business activity, costs are business expenses and should be budgeted for as with any other expenses. Make sure you allocate sufficient budget to build and maintain memberships of organizations and networks.

If your budget is limited, be creative in finding other ways to join. Some organizations give discounts or waive the membership fee if you become active on their board or in committees, as a token of their appreciation for your voluntary work.

Step 7: Beware of mismatch

If you attend a meeting of the Chamber of Commerce or alumni club of your university, it is unrealistic to expect that you will receive many requests for appointments the next day. Building relationships takes time. It depends on good preparation and active follow-up after the first contact. Your network has value if you regularly have contact with members outside of official meetings and if it brings you vital information, clients, and new jobs.

If you spend lots of time in a network without receiving anything back, assess if you have to adjust your expectations of this network and, consequently, the time you will devote to its activities. Some of the reasons for the mismatch may be that the network consists of people you have little rapport with (due to unbridgeable differences in backgrounds, industry, or level), who have little to give (no decision-making power), or who take more time to get acquainted than you expect. Other reasons might be that your follow-up was not adequate and people quickly forgot you because of this. Three main factors determine the strength of a network:

- The degree of emotional and business connections
- The possibility to reciprocate
- The frequency and form of communication.

A key question when you build your network is what value you can add for this person. Formulate your own goals in positive statements. If you are looking for a new job, emphasize the value you bring to any job instead of the reasons why you left your previous job.

Step 8: Organize the personal touch

Impressive are networkers who seem to remember exactly where you first met, what the topic of conversation was, and sometimes even what you were wearing. They give you the feeling that your story was interesting and that they spent time getting to know you. This personal touch is hard to resist, so you are inclined to more quickly accept a proposal from their side.

Professional strategic networkers have developed their method to leave nothing to chance. A contact about whom you know little more than the name and function on their business card is difficult to remember or introduce to another of your contacts; it is imperative you remember the person behind the card. Effective networkers do not just collect business cards but also focus on how their contacts can be of use to them or others in their network. There are many ways of organizing the personal touch:

- Discover how you remember people best: their name (so text on the business card); company (products, strategy); news fact (event); their personal appearance (hair, make-up, clothing, shoes); their favorite means of transport (make of car, color); their way of communicating (tone of voice, body language, smiling, jokes), or common interests (hobby, friends).

- Create your own system to capture the uniqueness of the person related to their potential value in symbols or text.

- Install a card-filing system on your computer. Use specialized software to scan business cards instead of copying the data and to ensure links to email and label-writing software, for example.

- Develop useful categories to store your labelled (symbols) business cards. Categories relate to your career priorities for the short and long term. If you are looking for a job or expect to have to look for a new employer next year, create a category 'new job'. In this category file all the business cards of people working at the companies you are interested in exploring opportunities with. Also file in this category the name cards of executive search firms and training bureaux for interview training or training in specific expertise you will need for your new job. If it is your ambition to work at a non-governmental organization (NGO) in Africa in the future, create the category 'Africa' and file in it all relevant contacts with people from comparable NGOs, intercultural communication trainers, and, for instance, contacts at development aid organizations and government departments. If you aim for a non-executive board position, file relevant contacts under 'NED', such as names of non-executive directors, specialists in corporate governance, lobby groups, accountancy firms, lawyers in the field, executive searchers, and so on.

- Use the categories as a search system when you need information or when you want to connect one of your contacts with someone of relevance in your database.

- Regularly update the categories and business cards to prevent overload.

Step 9: Focus on follow-up

Excellence in follow-up distinguishes the amateur networker from the professional. The first rule is to always keep your promises. If you promise to send someone information, an article or link, make sure you do this right away. A network works because of a bond of trust and respect between the members.

If the correct follow-up is impossible, make the effort to inform the person properly and timely. The best strategy is always to 'under-promise and over-deliver'. Since networking is a professional activity, make sure you apply the same standards to the follow-up as to your regular work. A good way to find the right tone for your follow-up is to ask yourself if this person would want to hire you in case of a vacancy.

Step 10: Use your networks strategically

Effective networking can be undermined by several factors:

- Too many contacts with similarities such as the same interests, background, and industry. The absence of diversity limits the potential of new ideas and viewpoints
- Too many close or personal relationships, such as friends, family, and direct colleagues
- Over-reliance on a very few people, with the risk of overcharging them
- Abusing your contacts by not properly thanking them if they provide you with an introduction or keep you informed
- Lack of reciprocity, leading to excessive time and effort invested from your side.

The effective strategic use of your network depends on three pillars:

- *Consistency of your message*
  Make sure that your highly valued contacts are confronted with one clear message from you in your introduction story and your follow-up. If you are looking for another job, emphasize your strong points and continue to present yourself as competent and professional in all communications with your contact. This will increase the chances that your contact will immediately remember you when a suitable vacancy is brought to his or her attention. Mixing messages makes it more difficult for people to remember you clearly.

- *Reciprocity in contact*
  Make sure your contacts feel their efforts are welcome and appreciated. Be prepared to offer something of value in return since this will create the best possible bond. Establish a 'bank account' in your mind, keeping track of the favors you have done and have asked. A commonly observed pattern in women is that they tend to give more than they ask for. Undervaluation of your network contacts can seriously harm your career. The ability to appreciate the potential value of your contacts and the courage to use them appropriately are key success factors in achieving top positions. Senior executives often receive more requests for introductions into their networks than they can handle. Therefore, you need to make sure that your request stands out because of the relationship you have built with them beforehand.

- *Careful follow-up*
  Follow-up is the glue of the network. Without it, your collection of business cards will remain just that. Trust and loyalty will only be reciprocated if given first.

Key factors for successful strategic networking

In summary, the four key success factors of strategic networking are as follows:

1. Know where you want to be in five years' time.
2. Networking is working.
3. Organize the personal touch.
4. Respect reciprocity by following up properly.

10.3 FAQs

Knowledge represents power. In decision-making processes in organizations there is a formal hierarchical framework in which official decisions are taken. On the other hand, informal networks may provide additional data that are important for the decision. Informal networks can extend very widely and, for instance, include your previous colleagues at a company you worked for or connections at the soccer club. Crucial decisions about individuals, such as those made during layoffs and promotion rounds, are often taken after wide information sources have been used to complete the picture. One of the most frequently asked questions relates to this working of networks: Why am I the last one to know when a crucial decision has been taken? Why was I not involved in the decision-making process?

Why am I always the last one to know?

Description

The hierarchical structure in a consultancy firm consists of many layers and functions. The share of women in the lowest layer is around 50 percent and in the highest 5 percent. The advancement of women to senior management positions has been designated a structural problem for which the company has developed a policy. Part of this policy is to stimulate partners to bring forward female candidates for promotions to senior levels.

One of the female senior managers intends to put forward for promotion one of her female managers. Despite her questions around the criteria, procedural issues and timing, she does not receive clear answers. Since business is booming, she does not have time to find out how proposals should be made and settles for sending a letter of recommendation to the responsible partner. Then she suddenly discovers that the list of promotions has already been published. Her candidate is obviously not on the list.

Analysis

Different elements play a role in this case study. First of all it is remarkable that the senior manager is not familiar with at least the formal procedures for promotions in the company. This may be caused by an absence of good connections with the HR department that generally coordinates these processes. Without fulfilling the necessary formalities, a proposal for promotion has little chance of success. It is rather naïve to be taken by surprise in a corporate culture in which politics play an important role.

This case study may be illustrative of certain organizational cultures in which it is an unwritten rule that proposals for promotions are done collectively and not by an individual manager. Sometimes this is related to responsibilities for reaching sales targets or an informal rotation scheme indicating whose candidate is up for promotion. In such a system, promotions are not always given to those with the best results and performance, but to those whose senior manager holds the decisive vote. Senior managers who operate outside the informal structure find that they have difficulty discovering the necessary information when they want to put forward their candidate.

A third element in the case study is the informal network's influence. Often, decisions are already known through the grapevine before being officially published. The fact that the senior manager was surprised about the announcement indicates that she was not part of any of the necessary informal structures.

Strategies

Informal networks are indispensable

Identify which informal networks exist and which characteristics
are shared by their members. Within companies there are networks of university alumni, but also previous project team members may continue to be in close contact. The connection could originate outside, for example as a result of living in the same neighborhood or sharing the same school for the children. Investigate where relevant groups meet and how they exchange information. Strong informal networks often even survive mergers and acquisitions. They remain intact long

after the integration of business units, and their members are referred to as coming from different 'blood groups'. It may take a generation before the networks disappear, only after their most senior members have retired or left the company.

Mentoring as a tool

Access to informal networks usually takes place through personal introductions by members. Asking for an introduction is not very successful and often leads to denial of its existence. A proven way to integrate into informal networks is to enter into mentoring relationships. Many companies have started mentoring programs in which senior male executives become mentors to aspiring female high potentials.[3] The mentoring sessions are beneficial to both parties. On the one hand, the women gain understanding of the unwritten rules of engagement in the organization. On the other hand, the mentor develops an understanding of the issues female managers struggle with. After a bond of trust and respect has developed between mentor and mentee, the mentor might introduce the mentee to some of the informal connections. The mentor might also promote the good name of the mentee by bringing it forward when names are solicited for promotions or interesting projects. In addition, the mentor might introduce the mentee to an outside connection of importance for her career. Similar effects can be observed in the acclaimed UK FTSE 100 Cross-Company Mentoring Program,[4] which effectively links senior women executives with chairmen and CEOs of listed companies.

In case your organization does not have formal mentoring programs it is advisable to actively approach senior executives with the request to serve as mentor. Most senior managers appreciate the invitation and are willing to invest in a business relationship provided its goals are clearly established upfront. In addition, the mentor needs to see added value in the relationship too in order to realize reciprocity in learning. Without clear goals and reciprocity a mentor session might develop into 'having a coffee and a chat', which is time-consuming and unproductive. Investigate beforehand what you have to offer a mentor and make reciprocity one of the key topics to discuss during your first session.

Why am I losing good clients to colleagues?

Description

A manager at an international law and accounting firm has recruited a new important client with a request for advice in a field she is not a specialist in. As a generalist in law, she is able to address the issue appropriately but her professional attitude commands her to refer the manager to an expert of another business unit working down the hall. A few weeks later she finds out that the specialist colleague failed to contact the client and just handed it to his roommate who was a generalist like her. He failed to contact the client immediately since he was overwhelmed with work for other clients.

When she contacts the client he expresses his annoyance with this unprofessional way of dealing with his question. She apologizes for the miscommunication. Because her colleague already started working with him it is not in the client's interest for her to take back the case now.

During her annual assessment she mentions having recruited a new important client for the firm but nobody seems to remember she brought him in. She is not allowed to record it on her assessment form nor does she score any points toward her promotion.

Analysis

The manager clearly acted in the best interests of the client and the company as a whole and not for her personal gain or glory. She put the client first in her quest to find the right expertise in the organization. Unfortunately, this was not acknowledged nor recorded officially, which might hinder her upcoming promotion. Some aspects in the case study indicate she missed out on crucial information which is present in informal networks.

- Often the unwritten rule exists that you do not give away a client or assignment to another business unit. Even if you are not the best-qualified person for the assignment, all efforts should be made to keep the client within your own business unit. The manager was not abreast of this unwritten rule and violated it. She should have worked with the client herself.

- Another unwritten rule is that if you do another business unit manager a favor by referring a client, your business unit should benefit from the referral too. Referring clients to others does not create respect with your unit colleagues. Only if the expertise required is very specialist and impossible to deliver in your own unit may you exchange the client with another client or project from the other business unit.

- A third unwritten rule is that putting the interest of the client or the company as a whole above the interest of your business unit is not always the best strategy for your career advancement.

- The fact that the manager only discovered the turn of events many weeks later indicated that she may not belong to the inner circle in her own unit or the company as a whole, since handling new clients is always discussed informally.

A similar case is the situation of a former politician who was a partner at a consultancy firm. She was very successful in recruiting new clients from her large network of political contacts. After many years of enjoying her role she found out that as time went by gradually all her new clients were transferred to other partners in the firm without her knowledge. The lack of support in the informal network made it possible for others to pass her over, which led to her leaving the company a year later.

Strategies

It is clear that building and expanding your formal and informal networks is crucial to prevent similar situations from happening. Networks ensure that you learn the unwritten rules in the company. They provide you with tools to create reciprocity with other business units and points for your own promotion. A large powerful network creates staying power and gives you a competitive advantage since you are informed better and in more timely fashion about critical issues.

Create leverage

Use 'giveaway clients' to create leverage in your network. Key to successful strategic networking is reciprocity. By placing value on your 'giveaway clients' others in your network will be inclined to give back other items of value at a certain point in time.

Networks as information channels

Integration in company's networks guarantees a flow of information about formal and informal events in the company.

Why do they decide for me?

Description

An experienced female marketing and sales director in a large international pharmaceutical company was proud of her excellent networking skills. During her 20 plus years on the job she had built up an extensive network of contacts in the company. Almost all managers knew her personally and she frequently worked with them to solve operational problems. Her excellent network enabled her to provide service and promotional materials of the highest quality and to become recognized as a top marketer. Her results were in line with expectations, and the executive board regularly praised her qualities. Therefore, she was completely surprised when a radical reorganization plan was announced, resulting in a transfer of a major part of her activities to local management teams. Her role would be limited to overall coordination at group level. She wondered why she had not been involved in the decision-making process.

Analysis

In this case study the networking qualities of the director were excellent, but the direction in which her network expanded needed improvement. Building and maintaining contacts aimed at solving operational issues is the basis for the execution of your function. But in order to keep abreast of strategically important developments, contacts outside the company – with stakeholders, shareholders, supervisors, industry groups, and so on – are essential. If she would have listened to these outside connections she would have known that the market was undergoing significant changes due to the speed of technological innovations driven by competition from Asia. As a result of the changing playing field, a radical change in corporate structure became imperative. Because she had not concentrated on her external networks, she missed crucial information and was confronted with the outcome.

Strategies

Develop strategic networking skills

Networking is only strategic if the starting point and goal are clear and business-related. Strategic networking is a tool to develop power inside and outside the organization through the exchange of knowledge relevant to your career. Without clear goals and business motives, maintaining connections becomes just a pleasant social activity.

SUMMARY SCHEDULE: PATTERN OF POWER, PERFORMANCE, AND PROMOTION

The following summary schedule provides an overview of the FAQs in Chapter 1 that relate to the pattern of power, performance, and promotion (Chapter 3). Some questions are explored through case studies that feature in Chapters 5–10. The number in brackets indicates where in this book the case studies can be found.

FAQ	Power	Performance	Promotion
Frameworks and culture			
Why am I treated as 'wife of' instead of business professional? (5.4)	Unknown in informal networks	Professional achievements unknown	Absence of professional image so prejudices take over
Why do they address me as secretary or assistant? (5.4)	Unknown in informal networks	Professional achievements unknown; focus on simple tasks	Absence of professional image so prejudices take over
Culture			
How do I manage cultural resistance? (6.3)	Build network for information and getting things done	Excellent performance as basis	Use network to promote yourself
Power and politics			
Why is someone else proposing my idea? (7.4)	Insufficient informal support and authority to be heard	Potential absence of track record in the area of your idea	Lack of preparation for meeting; no support built up
Why am I not being heard if I present my idea in the management team?	Lack of support in informal networks	Performance not in order or unknown	Absence of good name
How come some colleagues get away with everything?	Impact of staying power	Excellent performance as basis	Excellent reputation and name recognition

(Continued)

FAQ	Power	Performance	Promotion
Why do they ask me to deliver bad news? (7.4)	Lack of effective network that protects you	Excellence in female qualities working against you	Insufficient visibility as an all-round manager
Why do I suffer personal attacks? (7.4)	Lack of powerful network connections	Too much focus on execution	Absence of important external networks and good reputation
Why do I lose my job in the reorganization? (7.4)	No timely warning due to lack of informal network	Insufficient insight into qualities and value	Lack of promotion of qualities and value
Why do I miss out on the most favored positions? (7.4)	No timely information due to lack of network	Too much focus on execution	Lack of professional image
Career			
Why did I miss this promotion? (8.2)	Lack of information and support due to lack of network	Results not in line with (un)written expectations; perception of not being qualified	Ambition insufficiently communicated
Why do I not get the credit I deserve? (8.2)	Lack of network and support	Too much focus on executive tasks; executing tasks which are not yours	Insufficient self-promotion
Why do they always ask me for supporting instead of leading roles? (8.2)	Lack of network	Too much focus on supporting and executing tasks	Insufficient communication of your ambition
Which courses or studies do I need to take?	Alumni club as important factor	Related to performance in future role	Promotion as professional
Why do they often approach me for difficult tasks? (8.2)	Lack of network to protect you	Excellent performance used against you; difficulty saying 'no'	Insufficient promotion of your ambitions
How do I successfully land a board position? (8.2)	Informal network key to support and information	Excellent performance related to future role	Create relevant visibility for future role
Why do executive searchers never call me?	Lack of network (promotion of good name)	Lack of appealing results	Lack of visibility as a professional

(Continued)

FAQ	Power	Performance	Promotion
Skills			
Why is it so difficult to get back on track after a break?	Loss of relevant business networks	Past performance prevails	Image of not being committed
Why do I need to work so hard to get things done?	Lack of networks	Focus on execution; lack of delegation skills	Lack of professional image
Why do I not receive what I am asking for? (9.2)	Lack of information due to lack of networks	Too much reliance on execution	Lack of professional image
Why do I get remarks about my appearance? (9.2)	Lack of network for protection	Lack of professional performance	Lack of image so prejudices take over
How do I promote myself without provoking resistance? (9.2)	Via informal networks	Excellent performance as basis	Promote through stories and others
Why am I never the exception to the rule?	Lack of lobbying power	Insufficient knowledge of own capabilities	Lack of image; lack of name recognition
Why do I earn less than my male peers?	Lack of lobbying power and informal network	Too much focus on execution; lack of extra performance	Inadequate promotion of ambitions
What do I say when I suddenly come across our CEO in the elevator?	Prepare with information in informal networks	Present appealing results for company	Elevator pitch at hand
Networking			
Why is networking so important? (10.3)	Creates power	Enables excellent performance	Channels image-building
Why am I always the last one to know? (10.3)	Lack of information due to lack of informal network	Insufficient performance or performance not widely known	Lack of professional image
Why am I losing good clients to colleagues? (10.3)	Lack of knowledge of unwritten rules due to lack of informal network	Too much focus on execution	Lack of professional image
Why do they decide for me?	Lack of information and protection	Too much focus on execution	Lack of image and name
Why do I feel so uncomfortable at a business reception with all men in gray suits?	Lack of network to offer	Lack of appealing performance	Elevator pitch at hand

NOTES

Acknowledgments

1. http://ec.europa.eu/social/main.jsp?langId=en&catId=418&newsId=133& furtherNews=yes.
2. http://circa.europa.eu/Public/irc/markt/markt_consultations/library?l=/ company_law/institutions_remuneratio/individuals/inclusive_leadership/_ EN_1.0_&a=d.
3. http://www.youtube.com/watch?v=jHEL3hM35IQ.

2 Personal Leadership

1. Antoine De Saint-Exupéry (1984) *The Wisdom of the Sands*. Chicago: University of Chicago Press.

3 Pattern of Power, Performance, and Promotion

1. V. Kumra Singh and S. Vinnicombe (2002) 'Gender and impression management: playing the promotion game', *Journal of Business Ethics*, 37: 77–89.

4 The Female Leadership Paradox

1. R. J. Ely (1994) 'The effects of organizational demographics and social identity on relationships among professional women', *Administrative Science Quarterly*, 39 (2): 203–38.
2. 'The Seven Sisters' refers to seven liberal arts colleges in the north-east of the United States that are historically women's colleges, founded between 1837 and 1889. Today, the remaining five schools refer to themselves collectively as 'The Sisters'.
3. A. H. Eagly, M. C. Johannesen-Schmidt, and M. L. van Engen (2003) 'Transformational, transactional and laissez-faire leadership styles: A meta-analysis comparing women and men', *Psychological Bulletin*, 129 (4): 569–91.

4. S. Moore, L. Grunberg, and E. Grunberg (2005) 'Are female supervisors good for employee job experiences, health and wellbeing?', *Women in Management Review*, 20 (2): 86–95.

5. *Financial Times*, October 1, 2006.

6. September 16, 2008 at EuropeanPWN Round Table; www.europeanpwn.net.

7. H. Ibarra and O. Obadaru (2009) 'Women and the vision thing', *Harvard Business Review*, January: 62–70.

8. N. J. Adler (1996) 'Global women political leaders', *The Leadership Quarterly*, 7 (1): 133–61.

9. M. R. Thompson (2002) 'Female leadership of democratic transitions in Asia', *Pacific Affairs*, 75 (4): 535–55.

10. M. K. Ryan and S. A. Haslam. (2005) 'The glass cliff: Evidence that women are over-represented in precarious leadership positions', *British Journal of Management*, 16: 81–90.

11. www.regjeringen.no/en/dep/bld/Topics/equality/rules-on-gender-representation-on-compan.html?id=416864# (accessed December 19, 2010).

12. European Commission Database of Women and Men in Decision-making 2010; www.ec.europa.eu.

13. R. B. Adams and D. Ferreira (2008) *Women in the Boardroom and Their Impact on Governance and Performance*; http://ssrn.com/abstract=1107721: 1–44.

14. A. Kotiranta, A. Kovalainen, and P. Rouvinen (2007) 'Female leadership and firm profitability', *EVA Analysis*, 3 (Finnish Business and Policy Forum EVA).

15. See note 13.

16. M. Huse (2006) 'Gender-related boardroom dynamics: How Scandinavian women make and can make contributions on corporate boards', *Women in Management Review*, 21 (2): 113–30.

17. S. Nielsen and M. Huse (2010) 'The contribution of women on boards of directors: going beyond the surface', *Corporate Governance: An International Review*, 18 (2): 136–48.

18. V. W. Kramer, A. M. Konrad, and S. Erkut (2006) *Critical Mass on Corporate Boards: Why Three or More Women Enhance Corporate Governance*. Wellesley Center for Women's Publications: www.wcwonline.org/pubs/title.php?id=487.

19. C. Rose (2007) 'Does female board representation influence firm performance? The Danish evidence', *Corporate Governance*, 15 (2): 404–13.

20. O. C. Richard, T. Barnett, S. Dwyer, and K. Chadwick (2004) 'Cultural diversity in management, firm performance, and the moderating role of entrepreneurial orientation dimensions', *Academy of Management Journal*, 47 (2): 255–66.

21. J. A. Chatman and F. J. Flynn (2001) 'Being different yet feeling similar: The influence of demographic composition and organizational culture on work processes and outcomes', *Administrative Science Quarterly*, 44 (5): 956–74.
22. S. H. Glover, M. A. Bumpus, G. F. Sharp, and G. A. Munchus (2002) 'Gender difference in ethical decision making', *Women in Management Review*, 17 (5): 217–27. Also R. Loo (2003) 'Are women more ethical than men? Findings from three independent studies', *Women in Management Review*, 18 (4): 169–81.

5 The Power of Frames

1. J. E. Russo and P. J. H. Schoemaker (1990) *Decision Traps*. New York: Fireside, Simon & Schuster.
2. Gender pay gap is the difference between average gross hourly earnings of male paid employees and of female paid employees as a percentage of average gross hourly earnings of male paid employees. The population consists of all paid employees aged 16–64 that are at work 15+ hours a week (source: Eurostat).
3. M. C. B. Visser (2005) 'Women expatriates. What do you do all day?', *The Xpat Journal*, March–May: 46–7.

6 Culture

1. © Centre for Inclusive Leadership; see www.centreforinclusiveleadership.com.
2. A. H. Eagly (2005) 'Achieving relational authenticity in leadership: Does gender matter?', *The Leadership Quarterly*, 16: 459–74.
3. As at May 2010.
4. Apply the Pareto principle or law of the very few: around 80% of participants will be convinced, 20% will never accept it.

7 Power and Politics

1. L. L. Carli (1999) 'Gender, interpersonal power and social influence', *Journal of Social Issues*, 55 (1): 81–99.
2. C. T. Fong and L. Z. Tiedens (2002) 'Dueling experiences and dueling ambivalences: Emotional and motivational ambivalence of women in high status positions', *Motivation and Emotion*, 26 (1): 105–21.
3. OECD (2010) 'The effects of the crisis on unemployment'; www.oecd.org.

8 Career

1. See section 4.3.
2. Glass escalator describes men's success in rising to leadership positions in female-dominated groups, organizations, professions, and industries. Glass borders relate to the barriers for women to land international assignments.
3. C. L. Ridgeway (2001) 'Gender, status and leadership', *Journal of Social Issues*, 57 (4): 637–55.
4. A. H. Eagly and L. L. Carli (2007) 'Women and the labyrinth of leadership', *Harvard Business Review*, 85 (9): 62–71.
5. K. S. Lyness and K. Thompson (2000) 'Climbing the corporate ladder: Do female and male executives follow the same route?', *Journal of Applied Psychology*, 85 (1): 86–101.
6. P. Cappelli and M. Hamori (2005) 'The new road to the top', *Harvard Business Review*, 83 (1): 25–32.
7. Catalyst, 'The Bottom Line: Connecting Corporate Performance and Gender Diversity', www.catalyst.org; McKinsey (2007) 'Women Matter', www.mckinsey.com.
8. The Conference Board of Canada (2002) 'Women on boards. Not just the right thing ... but the "bright" thing'.
9. European Commission Database of Women and Men in Decision-making (2010); www.ec.europa.eu.
10. Further recommended reading: P. Thomson and J. A. Graham (2008) *A Woman's Place in the Boardroom – The Roadmap*. Basingstoke: Palgrave Macmillan.
11. The Sarbanes–Oxley Act is an American federal law of 2002, applicable to public companies listed at the New York Stock Exchange, which set new or enhanced standards for responsibilities of corporate boards.
12. J. Westphal and I. Stern (2007) 'Flattery will get you anywhere (especially if you are a male Caucasian): How ingratiation, boardroom behavior, and demographic minority status affect additional board appointments at U.S. companies', *Academy of Management Journal*, 50 (2): 267–88.
13. For instance, the activities of the European Professional Women's Network, such as the bi-annual EuropeanPWN Board Women Monitor and the Board Room Round Tables (www.europeanpwn.net).
14. European Commission Database of Women and Men in Decision-making (2010); www.ec.europa.eu.

9 Skills

1. Eurostat 2010; http://epp.eurostat.ec.europa.eu/.
2. Equality and Human Rights Commission UK (2009) *Financial Services Inquiry*.

3. L. Rudman. 'Self-promotion as a risk factor for women: The costs and benefits of counter-stereotypical impression management', *Journal of Personality and Social Psychology*, 74 (2): 629–45.

4. C. Watson and L. R. Hoffman (1996) 'Managers as negotiators: A test of power versus gender as predictor of feelings, behaviour, and outcomes', *Leadership Quarterly*, 7 (1): 63–85.

5. L. A. Barron (2003) 'Ask and you shall receive? Gender differences in negotiators' beliefs about requests for a higher salary', *Human Relations*, 56 (6): 635–62.

6. M. C. B. Visser and A. Gigante (2007) *Women on Boards Moving Mountains*. Paris: EuropeanPWN, 43–56.

10 Strategic Networking

1. 'Joining the club', *The Economist*, June 25, 2009.

2. I. J. Van Emmerik (2006) 'Gender differences in the creation of different types of social capital: A multilevel study', *Social Networks*, 28: 24–37.

3. M. C. B. Visser (2007) 'Mentoring women for corporate success. Case study ABNAMRO Bank', *Mentoring – A Powerful Tool for Women*. Paris: EuropeanPWN, 58–81.

4. FTSE 100 Cross-company Mentoring Program: www.praesta.co.uk.